THE BATTLE OF
SHEE ATIKÁ

RODGER BOLLES

Editor: Rebecca Bender

"May the words of this story fall upon you lightly as eagle down."

The Battle of Shee Atiká

Rodger Bolles

Editor: Rebecca Bender

Print ISBN: 978-1-48359-648-8
eBook ISBN: 978-1-48359-649-5

INTRODUCTION

FIRST CONTACT

"Mark four."

"Drop anchor."

"A fine anchorage," Dementiev observed.

"It is well protected. I thought I saw smoke," Chirikov replied. He slowly exhaled. He sailed the *Saint Paul* from Petropavlovsk, on the Kamchatka Peninsula, across the uncharted North Pacific to America's northwest coast. Not a man was lost, nor was there significant damage to the ship.

Forested islands broke a pelagic swell sheltering the anchorage. To the northwest a snow-capped mountain stood watch at the entrance to the sound. Captain Chirikov noted tall, straight spruce growing in abundance and resolved to survey the ship's spars. Eager to explore this dense coastal range, he sought fresh water, meat, and greens. The sun set on the Pacific coast of Alaska as the sea, forest, and mountains merged in twilight. An anchor watch was posted.

That evening Captain Chirikov made an entry in the ship's log:

Date: July 16, 1741

Time: 19:00

Lat.: 57° 03' North

Long.: 135° 8' West

Comments:

Anchored in four fathoms on clay bottom in an excellent bay marked by a singular mountain of the most beautiful and cone-shaped form I have ever seen. Abundant water and timber. As we entered the bay I noted smoke ashore.

At dawn Chirikov yelled from the quarterdeck, "Fleet Master Dementiev, take the pulling boat and ten armed men. Look for fresh water and spar timber close ashore. Rocks prevent landing but we will kedge in to provide cover. I saw smoke to the east. If you go out of sight, fire two shots when you land. Ensign Choglokov has some presents and barter items to use if you make contact with natives. Leave an armed man with the boat. Return before nightfall."

Dementiev and Choglokov disembarked with eight armed men.

"Keep your eye on that boat," the captain yelled to the main topmast.

The longboat pulled close ashore, then north along the coast, disappearing behind a tree-studded spit.

Chirikov smiled as he heard two pistol shots. The crew aired linen, mended, and washed their gear. The afternoon turned to dusk as the shore closed on the ship.

By the evening watch, the pulling boat had not returned. A soft, thick darkness cut the daylight short. Chirikov could smell the forest. He imagined he could hear it breathing: close, palpable, but unseen.

He fired shots, listening for a reply. They echoed emptiness. The watch lit blue signal lamps. All night, at two-hour intervals, the ship's cannon echoed off the surrounding mountains.

For six agonizing days Chirikov waited for a sign of those men before wind and weather drove his ship offshore and out to sea. They clawed their way back to the anchorage where, reluctantly, Chirikov sent the remaining boat with a carpenter and caulker on search and rescue. They rowed out of sight and disappeared. No shots were heard. The boats and crews were never seen again. Captain Chirikov sailed away. No European knew their fate. The Tlingit Kiks.adi, warriors of the rain forest, knew.

CHAPTER ONE

Cedar Man stirs and Xietl flies

While the handle of the Great Dipper is still visible, Xietl awakes. He stretches wings extending the length of four war canoes. He preens with monstrous claws and extends his wing talons. His black head is silhouetted by the rumbling volcanic glow of his roost. Hellish light reveals a long, sharp head, crested with great horns that sweep back from the crown. He moves to the edge of his eyrie atop Mt. Denali.

He leaps into predawn air too thin and cold for mortals. Thunder rolls with the downstroke of great wings, echoing far away to Shee Atiká.

Xietl soars over a chain of mountains formed by tectonic forces. Giant ice peaks and glaciers glisten white, pale blue, and pink in the dawning light. The great black specter glides above deep valleys where snow collects in winter and animals abound in summer. He flies over endless stages of smoking mountains, fire, and ice that tumble to a thunderous conjunction of the Arctic and rolling Pacific Ocean.

Volcanoes, earthquakes, tsunamis, and glaciers carve a snow-covered granite world, bearded in forest. Countless bays, inlets, and rivers lace the coast. An emerald necklace of islands protects the shore. Vortices of wind and rain sweep Shee Atiká Sound and into the woods. Lightning flashes from Xietl's glowing eyes as he scans the sea.

The village of Shee Atiká is on the rim of a sound overlooking protected waters. Beyond the village, at the foot of the mountains, is a rain forest. Mountain peaks form a semicircle towering over this winter village. There are six great houses ranked along a stony beach. Drying racks and canoes dot the shore. A totem pole, as tall as an old spruce, stands in front of the house called Eagle's Nest. Behind the row of post-and-beam houses stand the caches, bathhouses, and the birth hut. The village of the dead marks the edge of the forest. At the tree line are latrines and wood-gathering areas. A trail leads to a mountain stream.

The woods abound with fox, rabbit, beaver, bear, elk, and moose. Giant cedar and spruce anchor peat moss along streams full of salmon and trout. Gooseberries, strawberries, blueberries, and cranberries flourish in the thick undergrowth. Immense ferns and profuse wild roses adorn the moss-carpeted woods in this moist land warmed by a sea current from the east. The great blue sea abounds with whale, dolphin, sea lion, seal, sea otter, halibut, clams, crabs, and mussels.

Xietl espies Kit Yiyagu', and his talons pluck the killer whale from the sea. Kit Yiyagu' gashes one of Xietl's huge claws. Xietl's rage pierces the air and reverberates into the fjords ranging the sound. Through the mist, white thunder rumbles as glaciers cave into the sea. Xietl climbs as he circles over Shee Atiká. The blood of Xietl and Kit Yiyagu' mix, raining on a birth hut.

Qa-tla staggered through the storm to the creek and submerged his nephew in the clear, cold water. There was no outcry. "What? No strength," he mumbled. "If he dies, so be it. His body will float to the sea. The otter people will take him. Who wants a gaxtan?"

In a flash of lightning, Qa-tla saw ruby in the brown eyes of the baby. The wind swirled through the cedar and spruce, causing their branches to whistle and sway.

"Cedar Man stirs and Xietl flies. The spirit world lives, little one," Qa-tla told the baby. It was the beginning of the child's training. The lessons would be recited many times. The image of Xietl sat on top of a nearby totem pole. Its eyes glowed ruby red.

"Xietl must watch over us," said Qa-tla. "Long ago one of our leaders drowned at sea in a storm caused by Xietl's hunt of Kit Yiyagu'. Xietl gave us the right to his crest to atone. He will not let harm come to Eagle's Nest or even you, Gaxtan!

"See, Xietl sits atop the pole. His wings are spread while he faces downward. Kit Yiyagu' is grasped in his talons. Below Kit Yiyagu' is Eagle, and below him is Fog Woman. She holds a salmon in one hand and a copper shield in the other. At her feet are the first salmon she procured from her basket of fresh water in ancient times. She gave her salmon to the people in gratitude for Raven's lovemaking. Now Creek Woman, her daughter, lives at the head of every stream and brings the salmon back up the rivers each year in early fall.

"I'll tell you about the salmon. They rage upriver, battering their bodies against rocks while leaping over falls. They do not feed but will strike anything in anger. They change to a red color. The males' jaws curl, revealing ragged teeth. In a frenzy, they struggle to reach the spawning ground to breed and die. Their decaying bodies feed the hatchlings. The individual perishes, but the five clans of the salmon people, Chinook, Humpback, Chum, Coho, and Sockeye, live.

"See that totem pole, little one? Its name is Fog Woman Pole. All poles have names. This great symbol, this shrine, is a living being. Long ago a great warrior died. A giant straight cedar without knots was selected. From snow to snow they carved this pole. It was raised at a potlatch given by the son of the dead warrior to honor his father. While the pole was raised, the people danced and sang for three days and nights. The son gave all the people gifts. A slave was killed. They placed him on a log and pressed another against his neck to avoid marring his body. He would serve the warrior in the afterlife. A deep hole was dug for the pole. The slave's body was lowered into the hole. The pole was raised with ropes of cedar bark and supporting crutches. The people threw large rocks around the base of the pole so it would stand upright, and it still does."

Qa-tla again submerged the baby in the stream, calling out his name, Yaskadut, the name of his father. There was no cry. Qa-tla clucked his tongue, shaking his head in disappointment, and carried him back to the birth hut.

Tle'an straightened Yaskadut's arms to his sides and quickly wrapped him in a yard of white cloth made from the belly hairs of a mountain goat. Fresh moss was placed in the bottom of a carrier shaped into a cocoon. The baby's head rested on a feather pillow.

Tle'an, Yaskadut's mother, never let him cry. There were too many others in the house. When she worked, she placed him in a hammock made from the skin of a wolverine. It hung from the ceiling and could be rocked by pulling a string. It swayed gently as she softly sang and wove her baskets.

"He swings inside a wolverine skin. He will be strong and brave," Tle'an would say, as if repetition would make it so. While his mother gathered berries, Yaskadut was carried on her back, under a blanket secured by a belt. He would peek out or nap as she gathered the fruit. He was allowed the breast whenever he wanted it. Berries were chewed to a pulp for him.

By the end of the first winter, Yaskadut began to crawl out of the carrier. Gayu-tla fashioned an anklet for her nephew from the tendon of a wolf's hind leg.

"This will make him swift and strong. When he chases the bears and mountain goats, the alders will break over his shins." She smeared the slime from a recently killed bear's mouth on the boy. "This will make him brave," she said.

Since birth he wore an amulet, a beaded leather pouch that held his dried umbilical cord. When he had lived for three seasons, Qa-tla cut the cord of the amulet, announcing that Yaskadut was old enough to start becoming a man. He placed the amulet in an empty bear's den and yelled, "*Gax tl'tl*" (Cry luck) and "*At s'ati naxsiti*" (Master of the hunt let him become).

From the time Yaskadut was weaned, he was excluded from his mother's bed. Gayu-tla let him sleep under an eagle-down cover in her chamber. He ate whenever he was hungry and slept as he liked. If he made too much noise, he was told, "Keep quiet or the owl will come and take you away." He knew the story of the boy who was stolen by the owl and fed what he thought was delicious food, only to find that it was live insects that ate his insides.

Gaelgix, Tle'an, Gayu-tla, and Qa-tla all indulged him. They gave him costumes to wear at potlatches so he could dance and sing with the others. His uncle fenced a pond on the creek bank and made him a small canoe.

The children climbed rocks on the beach and waded in the ponds. Sometimes they dug holes in the sand, just big enough for their heads. They listened to the secrets of the surf. They picked flowers and paddled canoes. The girls played with dolls, little dishes, and pots. The boys played with small spears or bows and arrows. They all fished with hooks or gaffs. Wolf and bear cubs, baby seals, otters, and birds were their pets. They caught hummingbirds in berry jam, tied strings to them, and let them fly in circles.

Yaskadut was taught by parable, in the oral tradition of stories with moral lessons. He watched and imitated the practical skills of his elders. His uncle trained him to hunt, clean, and cook game. When his uncle asked him to fetch something, he would take a hot coal from the fire and say, "You must get it and return before this coal goes out or you will be lazy." If Yaskadut was too slow, the next time he was asked to do something, his uncle would say, "You are asking a lazy person," and everyone in the house would hear it. He was not allowed to sit around on rocks, because that would make him slow in the hunt. He could not "sit lazy," that is, sit with his legs stretched out in front of him. If he did this, some adult would come along and whack him on the shins with a stick. When he sat, he had to squat on his heels so that he was always ready to go quickly. Lying and stealing were so alien that they were deemed acts of witchcraft. A liar or thief could be tortured to death.

A bear had killed Yaskadut's father just before Yaskadut's birth. As was the custom, Qa-tla took Tle'an as one of his wives after his brother's death and became Yaskadut's provider, mentor, and disciplinarian. Yaskadut was forced to eat lots of fish and drink spoonfuls of oil rendered from the small oelachen fish. Yaskadut did not like the smell of the oil and complained that it was too greasy to swallow, but his uncle threatened to beat him if he did not. He explained that it was necessary to drink the oil to live through the cold winter.

Every morning, before the call of the raven, Qa-tla took him to the sea to bathe in the icy water. Yaskadut would tremble with the cold and turn blue. If he started to cry or tried to get out, his uncle would shout, "Stay in the water or I will beat you! You must become strong so that you will not die of the chest disease. Don't cry for your grandma or mother. They will not help you."

Once Yaskadut fainted from the cold and floated facedown. His uncle did not see it, but an eagle stooped with a shriek and struck Qa-tla in the head. Startled, Qa-tla glanced around, saw the boy, rescued him, and revived him by rubbing his body with snow. It was a strange occurrence; Qa-tla was reminded of Yaskadut's birth, Xietl, and the ruby eyes. Henceforth, he regarded the boy with awe, but continued his stern and rigorous training.

"You must learn to bathe without complaining," he told the boy. "All of your life will be better if you can stand pain without crying. Your enemy may torture and kill you, but he will respect you. You will respect yourself. The cold baths purify you. You must take such a bath before you hunt or go into battle, to be ready."

Yaskadut was not barrel-chested like the others; he was thin and willowy, but very quick. After nine seasons, he could run faster than anyone in the village. His weapons were courage and wit, but the bigger boys treated him with disdain. He had to fight to join the others in the bathhouse. It was the custom of the men, women, and children to bathe in age groups. Young men sat in the steam, then dove into the nearby cold river or rolled in the snow. Old men gathered in the bathhouse to tell stories. It was in the bathhouse that Yaskadut learned how his father, also called Yaskadut, died. Ol' Galweit told of the bear hunt.

CHAPTER TWO

The Voyage of the Neva

Stars of the second magnitude glimmered through the mist. A steady breeze followed throughout the day. At sunset, a meteor appeared below the North Star. Its fireball lit up the ship for thirty seconds, while the wake remained for an hour.

The night watch came on as the ship's bell measured the somnolent rhythm of creaking wood and hemp. The *Neva* rose and fell on the breast of a following sea. Rigging groaned in pad eyes as a drifting halyard slated. The moan of wood, canvas, and line swayed the sailors to sleep.

Jade foam curled before the bow, cascading moonlit emeralds and lace. The ship climbed meadows of rolling seas. Dolphin, gamboling in a luminescent wake, sped by in formation to ride the bow wave. One rolled onto his back, pierced the sea, and rose fifteen feet into the air, dead off the bluff bows. He hung suspended, nodded to Yurii, then skimmed under the starboard bow. The *Neva* made seven knots on a swaying broad reach.

Yurii Lisianski relaxed as he recalled the events that had led to this moment. He remembered the dinner with Tsar Alexander the Great in detail. The guests included the imperial family, the government ministers, and many prominent learned men. The occasion was used to announce the elevation of Count Nikolai Petrovich Rezanov to the rank of High Chamberlain.

The dinner commenced with hors d'oeuvres in an anteroom near the entry to the Great Hall. Guests chatted and grazed at the buffet graced with decanters of various flavored vodkas, chilled crystal glasses, and ice sculptures. Slices of savory sturgeon, salmon, ham, salami, roast fowl, and cheeses covered the tables. Platters of cold poached sturgeon with horseradish sauce, salmon in aspic, pickled herring with mustard sauce, and jewels of pearl-gray beluga, golden sterlet, and jet-black sevruga caviar graced the small round tables. Marinated mushrooms, fruits, brined apples tossed with cranberries, pickles, and freshly baked white and dark breads completed the array.

Alexander the Great stood in the anteroom, resplendent in a white uniform trimmed in silver piping and a red sash as he addressed Anton Von Kruzenstern and Yurii Fedorovich Lisianski.

"Peter the Great was right: Mother Russia must establish a presence on the seas of the world," he said. "More immediately, we must use the sea route from St. Petersburg to Okhotsk to support our people in the Far East and Alaska. Every year we use more than four thousand horses to travel overland to that region. In some places summer brings great swamps where it is impossible to ride or walk, so one must wait for the winter. In others it is impossible to ride or walk due to deep snows. It takes years and is even more dangerous and expensive than sailing around the Horn or the Cape of Good Hope. We need more ships and men to sail upon the seas.

"There are vast resources to be exploited in our Far Eastern provinces. Our trappers provide revenue, and the indigenous people in that region must be comprehensively assimilated. We can bring them to God, health, and security in a respectful and dignified way. Unfortunately, we haven't done much in that area since Vitus Bering's expedition. We were diverted by our Orthodox friends in the Caucasus who needed help. Meanwhile the English, French, Spanish, and Americans all show interest in exploiting the Alaska coastal region.

"The Admiralty and I have something in mind. That is why you gentlemen were invited to dine with us. This is a celebration of the commencement of a great undertaking, one in which you two and the crews you select will represent Mother Russia. We want you to obtain two suitable ships, man them, and sail around the world, collecting information and establishing contacts along the way. Over all command of the expedition and the Russian-American Company in Kamchatka and Alaska will be Count Nikolai Petrovich Rezanov. He and his staff will sail on a frigate. That ship—we will call it the *Nadezhda*—will sail with a second, smaller vessel, which will be christened *Neva*. They will convoy from St. Petersburg to the North Pacific. The *Nadezhda* will proceed to Japan to establish diplomatic ties and trade after she and the *Neva* make a port call at Petropavlovsk, Kamchatski. The *Neva* will proceed to Baranov's fort in Kodiak. At a designated time, both vessels will rendezvous and convoy back to St. Petersburg. The details are spelled out in the written orders you will receive later this evening. We propose a trip like that of the great English captain, James Cook."

Yurii was thunderstruck. He knew he had been summoned for a commission to a ship but was amazed that this dream was being handed to him. He stood quietly alongside his classmate, whose German given name and patronymic, Johann Von, was russified into "Ivan Fedorovich," though he retained his family name of Kruzenstern.

The complex and illusive young tsar, who had been raised by his grandmother, Katherine the Great, bedazzled Yurii. He was honored just to stand in the same room with this star of European aristocracy. Alexander's philosophy included an exquisite affirmation of human dignity. His compassion and sensitivity were expressed in his speech and his manner.

Yurii was overjoyed to listen to his tsar on such an intimate basis. He was proud of his country, his tsar, and himself for being selected for this great venture. He resolved to dedicate all of his energy and his life, if necessary, to this voyage.

"I invited both of you to dine with me so we can discuss this further. Are you game, gentlemen?"

Both men answered in unison: "Yes, Your Majesty," and the party moved through the opening doors into the immense ballroom of Katherine the Great's Summer Palace. The ballroom was a white hall of crystal candlelight and golden appliqué, with floor-to-ceiling windows draped in white satin and glittering in silver wall mirrors. Inlaid floors of varicolored and intricate hardwoods stretched for one hundred yards. Overhead was a mural depicting Russia's history.

While a pianist played Beethoven's sonatas, the following menu was served:

Sterlet ukha, rice and egg pirozhki, was complemented by sherry, Madeira, marsala, and white port.

Beef hussar-style was accompanied by port, Médoc or Château Lafite Rothschild.

Sauternes, Rhine wine, Moselle, Chablis or white Burgundy was served with poached salmon in walnut sauce.

The buttery-lemon taste of hollandaise sauce was drizzled over poached asparagus, complemented by Malaga, Tokay, or Château d'Yquem.

Chilled cracked crab preceded roasted, stuffed grouse.

A lettuce salad with sour cream dressing cleansed the palate and aided digestion, as did dry French champagne bottled in crystal made especially for the tsar.

Wild strawberry cream, cheese, and fresh fruit concluded the feast.

Afterward, the ladies enjoyed coffee and tea or sherry in a garden room, and the gentlemen enjoyed cognac, rum, and liquors with Havana cigars before an immense fireplace in a book-lined study.

Alexander continued his conversation with Ivan and Yurii before the warm fire. "I suggest you engage the services of the master shipbuilder Rasumanov to help you select and fit out suitable vessels. He is the grandson of Gregory Rasumanov, who learned his trade in the Dutch shipyards alongside Peter the Great. This fellow is the third generation of shipbuilders in that family."

Not long after, Yurii and Rasumanov, who was called by his last name only, found themselves on the long coach ride from St. Petersburg to Calais. From there a boat trip would take them to the English shipbuilding port of Whitby.

Rasumanov asked, "Have you seen the mountain of stuff offered to take along?"

"Yes," Lisianski replied. "It is onerous, but most of it will be useful, and we cannot afford to offend such gentlemen and sponsors as Counts Stroganov and Rumiantsev."

"What are we going to do with those piles of books—Cadmus, Harmonious, and Poly-somebody? The devil knows what savages will do with Dmitriev's *Fables and Stories*!"

"Don't sell the fables short, Rasumanov. At birth *we* were little savages; those fables and stories helped civilize us. Stroganov's atlases and science texts will be useful to educate the natives in modern techniques of navigation, mechanics, and construction. But I confess I am not sure how they will react to the 'Objets d'Art' the Count sent along, not to mention Fuchs's giant portrait of General Suvorov."

"I am sure it is intended to instill awe in the minds of the savages," Rasumanov replied sarcastically.

"If they knew of our history, they would honor him," replied Yurii.

"Well, we must obtain two ships capable of hauling all this stuff, our gear, rigging, supplies, and crew, with enough room left for trade goods, specimens, and God knows what else. A life-size portrait of Suvorov takes up a lot of room."

"There is so much to consider when examining these proposed vessels. We failed to find suitable ships in Germany."

"May I ask what the English want for these two vessels, Yurii Fedorovich?"

"They have asked twenty thousand pounds sterling. We countered with seventeen thousand, contingent upon our approval of the vessels, after our survey. That does not include the five thousand set aside for refurbishing. By the way, what do you intend to do?"

"We will shorten the spares for the southern seas, add a cut-water, head and trail boards for flotsam and ice, raise the bulwarks the entire length, and add a poop and cabin with ornate stern. Insert the gun ports. Raise the heights of the channels and chain plates to spread the shrouds. That will make her shortened rigging even more stout. And of course we will convert the holds to accommodations."

They both fell silent as the coach raced through the night. They smoked, drank, slept, and ate in that coach. There was much to be done and time was short. It was vital to get away in the proper season.

After the morning halt and change of horses, Yurii continued the conversation.

"What are the specific dimensions of this *Thames*, Rasumanov?"

"She has been surveyed. I have drawings of the hull and sail plans that I will show you." He read from a page, "The English dimensions are these:

"Length on lower deck 97' 8"

"Length of keel for tonnage 81' 0"

"Breadth extreme 29' 2"

"Depth in hold 11' 4"

"Burthen in tons 368

"Aren't you interested in the *Leander*?" he asked.

"Not much. I know she is a 450-ton frigate. She will be rechristened the *Nadezhda*, and Ivan Fedorovich will captain her. I am more curious about my ship, the war sloop. She must carry a good sail."

"That requires a low center of gravity," replied Rasumanov. "She sits low in the water and her rigging is right. There is no topgallant mast fidded on the mizzen. The only square sail on the mizzen is a topsail. There are no royals or sky sails."

"We want her to steer well and to quickly answer the helm."

"She will keep a good wind, and she is a sharp ship, which is good for that, but she must also be capacious and take the ground while standing upright. Trade-offs were made, but she can be driven in excess of nine knots in ideal conditions—say with twenty-five to thirty knots of wind aft of beam."

"That is a good speed for this vessel."

"It is enough to sail around the world in a reasonable amount of time."

"She must carry her guns well out of the water."

"It was clear to me, sir, that your command could use a bark similar to the HMS *Endeavour*, the converted collier that Captain Cook employed for his circumnavigation in 1768 to '71. Of course, when Nikolai Petrovich arrives with his diplomatic entourage in Japan, it will be aboard a fully battle-ready frigate. That will be impressive."

"That is a different mission. We will be close ashore, collecting specimens and information. We need a ship that can be worked through the narrows, take a grounding without major damage, and sail short-handed, if necessary."

"That means a round bottom and stout construction with a simple sail plan. She has that. A round bottom will make her roll when the weather is abeam. We must see how she takes the seas."

"Captain Cook described the *Endeavour* as sufficiently stiff and remarkably easy in her rolling on great seas. That is why the *Thames* was recommended. She is a collier built in the Whitby yard of the master builder Thomas Fishburn, who built Cook's *Endeavour*. In his letter he describes the *Thames* — shall we call her by her new name, the *Neva*?" Yurii suggested as he continued reading from a letter. "'She is fitted with an impressive amount of canvas, including stun sails, long fore and main lower masts, and a very square appearance aloft. The mizzen is short, but the heel of the lower mast is stepped on a block supported on the keelson. This has the effect of raising the height of the crossjack yard. She is suitably capacious to stow the required provisions. The loading ports will be closed.' Of course," he added, "we need some means of self-defense."

"The spar deck will serve as the gun deck for fourteen Blomefield iron guns. Mountings for swivel guns will be fitted."

"That ought to do. They throw a six-pound ball one thousand yards. The English use them as chase guns on their sloops. What about the hull and the draft, Rasumanov?"

"I saw Cook's ship. She had quite pleasing lines for a bulk carrier. The *Neva* is a sister ship of the *Endeavour*. She has fairly flat floors, slight deadrise, full bilges, and vertical sides with a sudden tumblehome above. Her bow is a full bluff entrance with some concavity in the lower part. The run is concave. Draft is three meters."

"What about her accommodations?"

"Most are below on a five-foot deck, head to beam. There is more headroom in her great aft cabin, with four quarter-windows and a port sash window."

"What about her hull?"

"Her hull is double sheathed with oak. She has an elm keel and Baltic pine for her decks, topsides, masts, and spars. Her bottom is coated with a thick layer of white lead and grease to make her teredo-proof."

They fell silent as images of such a ship filled their thoughts. The coach traveled through the night.

In the morning, as they approached Whitby, Lisianski asked, "You've been to Whitby; what is it like?"

"Whitby is an ancient English fishing port with numerous shipbuilding yards. She sits on the North Sea at the mouth of the River Esk. A convenient quay runs through the middle of town. The place is thoroughly nautical. An abbey sits high above the town on a cliff and serves as a good landmark for an approach."

*   *   *

On June 5, 1803, the ships arrived at Kronstadt. Alexander the Great came aboard to inspect. Both Kruzenstern and Lisianski received the Order of Vladimir of the Third Class and annual pensions of three thousand rubles for life. Kruzenstern was concerned about the welfare of his new bride, and Alexander awarded her an estate that would produce 1,500 rubles per year for twelve years.

After the purchase of the ships and their sail to St. Petersburg, Lisianski purchased the ship's supplies and equipment. He selected suitable English clothes and undergarments for the vagaries of the weather. Supplies included straw mattresses, pillows, sheets, and blankets; biscuits made in St. Petersburg; and salt meat pickled in Hamburg. He was acutely aware of the ravages of scurvy and Captain Cook's phenomenal success in avoiding it, so he purchased such delectable antiscorbutics as portable soup, essence of malet, essence of fir or spruce, dried yeast, mustard, sauerkraut, and cranberry juice. In Copenhagen, while under way, he added tea, sugar, and eighty puncheons of brandy to the stores.

For small arms, he selected two dozen British military flintlocks. Weighing 9.75 pounds each, they were fifty-five inches in length and fired a 6.5-millimeter ball. These firearms supplemented the ships' Russian musket flintlocks. The latter were converted to percussion caps.

For navigation, Lisianski selected several top-quality sextants, direction-finding compasses, barometers, hydrometers, thermometers, Arnold and Pettington chronometers, two surveying compasses, many charts, and a lunar table.

The task was to cross the Atlantic, round the Horn, and sail the Pacific to Alaska. They would winter in Kodiak and proceed to Canton for fur trading. From Canton, they would sail via the Cape of Good Hope back to Kronstadt, completing the circumnavigation of the globe with the *Nadezhda*. Their duties included noting sea currents, temperatures, and bottom conditions, down to four hundred meters. They were to chart straits and harbors, log atmospheric pressures, make systematic astronomical observations, and enter accurate longitudes and latitudes for points of travel and geographic features. They were tasked with preparing descriptions, sketches, and charts of the land, with special emphasis on the Island of Kodiak and the shores of Alaska. The primary purposes of the voyage were to collect scientific data, establish trade, develop military intelligence, and resupply outposts in the Far East.

Lisianski chose not to enlist foreigners with sea voyage experience. Even though he and his fellow lieutenant-captain, Kruzenstern, were of equal rank, he preferred the latter play the role of commander of the ships in the Ministry of Marine Affairs. Lisianski was allowed to select his own crew.

Kruzenstern gave Lisianski the following written order of sail: "You are to make port at St. Julian on the coast of Patagonia and at Valparaiso on the coast of Chile as places of rendezvous in the event of separation on the sail across the Atlantic.

"After reaching St. Catherine, in the event of separation, you will cruise for three days off Cape St. John, the eastern point of Staatenland. If you do not see the *Nadezhda* in that period of time, continue to the harbor of Conception. Wait there fifteen days.

"In the event we are separated beyond Cape St. John, and you, on the twelfth of April, are advanced more to the northward than forty-five degrees and to the westward of eighty-five degrees, make for the port of Anna Maria on the Island of Nukahiva, one of the Washington Islands. Wait ten days for *Nadezhda*. But if on the twelfth of April, the *Neva* has not reached the parallel of forty-five degrees and the meridian of eighty-five degrees, make for Port Conception, take in a supply of water and refreshments with all convenient speed, and then steer directly to the Sandwich Islands, but not without touching at the group called Washington Islands, and inquiring after the *Nadezhda* in Port Anna Maria.

"In the event of complete separation, the ships are to sail to the Sandwich Islands. If they become separated, the *Nadezhda*, with its envoy, will sail on to Japan. She will winter in either Kamchatka or Kodiak. The *Neva* is to sail directly to the northwest coast of America, winter there, take on a load of furs, and return to Kronstadt by way of Canton, where she will sell her cargo."

The *Nadezhda* and the *Neva* moved out of Kronstadt Harbor into the roadstead on the morning of July 19, 1803. There they lay, trapped by contrary winds until the seventh of August. They restowed gear and made ready for the long voyage. Yurii was reminded of the old saw, "No matter how much time there is, a ship is never ready to sail on the day of departure."

CHAPTER THREE

Yaskadut, son of the Bear Slayer

Galweit was awake. He always rose early to rekindle the fire or start a new one. Using a thin hide strip to spin a cedar drill, he coaxed the fire until it burned brightly. The thick pallet of beach grass rustled as Gaelgix threw back her blue fox cover. She paused to wash her face in water kept in a bentwood box. Cradling the shallow limestone bowl of a seal oil lamp in her hands, she moved toward a glow in the fire pit at the center of the room. She entered a side room and nudged Gayu-tla. "Gayu-tla, wake up! You will die if Raven calls before you rise."

Gayu-tla groaned as she rolled from her bed. The cover shimmered with the blue, teal, and green of mallard feathers. She washed her face in cold water and retrieved a spruce root basket from a gut bag. The roots had been gathered, scraped, parboiled, and left to soak for weeks. Her copper weaving blade glistened in the morning fire as she worked to finish the basket.

Young men in breechcloths left the house to bathe in the sea and cut firewood. Old men dressed their grandchildren. Little girls played with clamshell imitations of their mothers' stone lamps. Boys ran outside to practice with small spears and bows and arrows while they waited for the first meal of the day. The house warmed with the crackling pit fire. Everyone munched smoked salmon. Gaelgix retrieved an ember and blew, touching the twisted grass wick in her lamp. Stars glittered through the smoke hole. She skirted the smooth river rocks defining the fire pit as she padded over worn planks to the benches lining the walls of the main room.

Gaelgix returned to the sleeping room she shared with Ol' Galweit. They had the honor of a room at the back of the house behind a screen bearing the crest of Xietl. Galweit's brother was the house chief, Yaskadut, the Bear Slayer. The chief's chambers were the most distant from the entrance. Fifty men, women, and children slept along the back and sides of the house, according to their status.

Gaelgix and Tle'an joined Gayu-tla as they worked on their baskets. The long rainy season marked the end of summer. It was the time for basket weaving.

"Tle'an, did you want a boy or a girl?" asked Gaelgix.

"I didn't care," replied Tle'an. "A boy will hunt. A girl will have babies."

Gayu-tla glanced at Gaelgix as she smiled. "What if it were neither?"

"That would have been all right. To have such a one in the house is good luck."

"Not for the wives," Gayu-tla giggled.

"How will the child be called?" Gaelgix asked.

Tle'an announced, "I named him Tcenio."

They all laughed at the thought of a boy named "Stinky."

"That is a nickname," Gaelgix said, "but what of a real name?"

"Well, of course, it is Yaskadut," replied Tle'an.

"That's good. He should be named after his father, Yaskadut, the Bear Slayer. It will be good to see Yaskadut again. He is a great hunter," nodded Gaelgix.

"If it were a girl?" prompted Gayu-tla.

"Then she would have been called Tle'an, after my mother."

The evening meal was smoke-dried fillets of halibut, skewered on sticks. The sticks were jammed into the ground next to the open fire. The flesh softened and basted itself. The broiled fillets were cut into chunks and dropped into a spruce root woven basket filled with a mixture of sea- and fresh water. Hot stones were placed within the basket to bring the water to a boil. Butter clams, mussels, rice root, and chopped beach lavage were added to the broth.

A salad of sea beach sandwort, sour dock leaves, fireweed, and wild cucumbers was offered with the fish stew. A jelly of boiled honey, agar, and wild raspberries completed the meal.

This sumptuous meal celebrated the end of summer and the beginning of a long stay in the winter house. Each member of the household brought his own elaborately decorated wooden bowl and a spoon made from a mountain sheep horn etched with figures of animals.

The weather had turned. Summer was gone and the long season of rain had started. The firewood was gathered and stacked. Great stores of food were cached in the storage wells. The fire pit warmed the house as they listened to the sounds of a heavy rain ushering in the winter season. The Tlingit turned their attention to household tasks, art, music, storytelling, dance, and romance. All was well.

Galweit announced that he would sing "Raven Cries for Daylight" to teach the children how Raven stole the daylight and gave it to the people. The song told this story:

"There was no light, no stars or moon. Then Yel heard that a house chief at the head of the Nass River held the sun, stars, and moon in boxes in his house. He decided to get them. So he went to the man's house and waited by the well. A slave was ordered by the chief to fetch water for his daughter to drink. Yel disguised himself as a feather and floated on top of a bucket of water. The chief saw the feather by the light of a pitch torch. He told the slave to dump it and go get some fresh water. Yel was promptly dumped on the ground, but he hid by the door. When the slave came back, Yel disguised himself as a pine needle, dropped into the bucket, and hid in a corner. The girl drank the water, swallowing the pine needle. She became pregnant, and gave birth to Yel reincarnated as a man-child.

"The grandfather loved the new baby very much and would give the baby anything he wanted. Yel spotted the boxes with the daylight, the moon, and the stars. He started crying for the box with the stars. The old man finally gave in, and Yel released the stars. A few days later, the baby cried to open the smoke hole so his grandfather could release the moon from its box. Then Yel cried for the box with daylight in it. The old man, just like all grandfathers, could not resist, and Yel took the box with daylight. He suddenly flew up through the smoke hole. Before he flew up the smoke hole, Yel was white; ever since then he has been shiny jet black. When he returns he will be snow white.

"Yel came to a river and demanded the people there take him across, or he would break daylight on them. They did not believe him, and when he did break daylight, the people scattered. Some were wearing sealskins, and they became seals. Some wore goatskins, some groundhog, some bearskin. They all became those animals."

After the song, Galweit decided to tell how the first white men came:

"I am old. I have lived many seasons, but I remember.

"Long ago some Tlingit drowned in their baidarka in the ocean. They had sea otter skins in a waterproof bag made of halibut skin. This bag sailed away to the land of the Anooshi. The Anooshi saw these sea otter pelts and came here on big ships.

"When the people first saw the ship coming, they were frightened. Some thought it was Raven coming back as he promised. He was white, just as he was before he flew up the smoke hole. People were afraid to look on Yel. Some said it was a great whale.

"People ran and hid in the forest. After a while, they started to peek out. They thought they would turn to stone if they looked directly at Yel. Some broke off pieces of blue hellebore stalk, poked holes through them, and looked through, to avoid being turned to stone. Others feared for their children, so they hung dog droppings and devil's clubs around the children's necks.

"No one knew what was coming. One old man who was almost blind said, 'I will go in my canoe and see. It does not matter if I die, because I am old.' This old man came back and said, 'This is a big canoe. People are in it.' Others went out to see. Some thought the creatures were button lobsters because they had buttons on their bellies and backs. Others saw them breathing smoke and thought they were monsters.

"A stench floated across the water, making the people sick. Later they learned that it was the smell of black tar smeared on the hull of the ship. Some young men went on board. They saw a box that held them in it, like the surface of still water. They were given food. It looked like maggots with white sand on it. They stared at it. They were told to eat it, so they took a bite. It was good. They were told it was rice with sugar. They drank something that burned and made them feel happy. Well, this is all."[1]

Tle'an recalled the birth scene: "Gaelgix! Gaelgix! Wake up. The baby comes," she announced as she shook Gaelgix's shoulder.

---

1   This is my amalgam of stories told by Charlie White and George Betts in *Haa Shuka', Our Ancestors, Tlingit Narratives*, Vol. 1, University of Washington Press (1987).

"Tle'an," whispered Gaelgix, "you must leave Eagle's Nest. We must go to the birth hut. Blood and afterbirth contaminate men and offend the spirits of the animals they hunt."

The hut was just large enough to accommodate Tle'an, Gaelgix, and Gayu-tla. They heated rocks in a small fire pit to keep the child and mother warm. A hole filled with fresh moss was in the center of the hut. Tle'an straddled this hole. She grasped a vertical pole in front of her. Gaelgix crouched behind, supporting Tle'an's buttocks with her knees as she held her shoulders. Gayu-tla held Tle'an by the waist and squatted in front of her. She braced her knees against Tle'an. When the pains came, Gaelgix said, "Pull on the pole and swallow your breath down." As each labor pain subsided, Tle'an rested on the knees of Gaelgix. She grasped the pole, held her breath, and bore down as Gaelgix pressed against the small of her back. Finally, the membrane broke and the water gushed. "Good. Only two or three more and the baby will be here," said Gaelgix. The baby slid smoothly onto the soft moss. Gayu-tla retrieved him while Gaelgix poured water onto hot rocks, filling the hut with steam. She grasped Tle'an about the waist and squeezed with each pain to help expel the afterbirth. Gayu-tla wrapped the afterbirth in a seal skin. She tied it into a little bundle resembling a man. She guided the baby's hand to knock over the little man. "See how strong he is. He will be a great warrior," she said. Gaelgix passed the baby through the entry to his paternal uncle, Qa-tla. The baby did not utter a sound. His eyes were bright and piercing. He had the unblinking stare of a raptor. Qa-tla examined the boy, noting that the limbs were slight and lean. He did not weigh much. His chest was narrow.

Qa-tla mumbled, "He looks like gaxtan, a girl-boy."

CHAPTER FOUR

Man Overboard

"Coming abeam of the guard-ship, sir."

Lisianski bespoke the deck officer, "Heave-to."

The officer yelled, "Brace fore and main yards 'gainst the wind. Mizzen yards aback."

The watch commander acknowledged the order. The crew executed it.

"Ahoy, the *Neva*. Admiral Hanikov requests permission to aboard."

"Permission granted. Stand by to receive boarding party."

The ship's afterguard and officers assembled to present arms as the admiral boarded at the entry port. He doffed his tricorner to the quarterdeck as the bosun piped him aboard.

"Captain Lisianski, congratulations. I see you are well under way. It is not my intention to delay your departure, but I could not resist wishing you well."

"Thank you, Admiral. The men and I appreciate this courtesy," replied Lisianski, struggling to disguise his impatience. "It is an honor to have you aboard. Please join me in my cabin for a farewell toast. Stand by, Lieutenant Povalishin. We will depart when the admiral takes his leave."

The captain and his guest went below, where Yurii poured two half-tumblers of Napoleon brandy. He raised his glass in toast: "To His Most Gracious Majesty, for making this voyage possible."

"Captain, I drink to you and the brave men who undertake this great voyage for the honor and glory of Mother Russia," Admiral Hanikov said with a wistful look in his rheumy eyes. "My day has come and gone, or I would be on board this vessel with you and damned glad."

"We shall remember your courtesy and assistance, sir."

"Thank you, Yurii Fedorovich. You have brightened the life of this old port admiral. I wish you a favoring breeze," he toasted, draining his glass.

*   *   *

Sails were shaken out from the fore, main, and mizzen. Jibs and topsails were set and braced.

While the ship sailed smartly on a larboard tack to sea, the officers and crew assembled. Lisianski spoke from the quarterdeck:

"We are undertaking a great enterprise for the glory of Tsar Alexander and Mother Russia. We will be the first Russian sailors to circumnavigate the globe. We will collect information and establish trade. Our voyage must serve as an example for those to follow. Courage, patience, and perseverance will be required. Great pleasure and benefit will come from cordiality with one another, due obedience to your superiors, and observance of perfect cleanliness in everything relating to both the ship and your persons. Nothing less will be admitted.

"Your rations will be as follows: To each man per day, one pound of meat, one pound of biscuit, and one glass of brandy. Each week you will receive a pound of butter, a mess of pea soup, a kasha or grit pudding, and a sufficient quantity of mustard and vinegar.

"That is what every man jack of you will receive, be he officer or seaman. You are the best that Russia has to offer and you will bring honor to her. Father Gideon will now give us a benediction."

On the thirteenth of August, 1803, the *Neva* cleared the Gulf of Finland. On the fourteenth, with the Isle of Gotland in view, tragedy struck at two bells.

"Man overboard! Man overboard!" a crewman yelled.

The deck officer bellowed, "Stand by to tack ship! Weather main and lee crojik braces! Come about!"

The main yards came around on the weather side and crojik on the lee. Lisianski gave orders to the wheel: "Hard a-lee. Steady now, hold 'er there, steady. Up a bit. Off a bit. Hard down, steady, hold 'er there." The *Neva* hove to.

The deck officer reported, "Seaman Epifanov fell overboard while drawing a bucket of water."

"Where away?"

"There! There! Where the bucket floats!"

"Lower a boat!"

A boat was lowered. The men searched for an hour. Finally, Lisianski reluctantly ordered the ship under way and retired to his cabin to conceal his anguish. *Бог знает что случилось! (God knows what happened!) What can I say to his family? It's odd … Body did not come up … Good swimmer … Must have hit his head. I wanted to bring them all back.*

"Not one more man shall die!" he shouted aloud to no one in particular.

Lisianski had handpicked all the crew. He knew their families. He had visited Epifanov's home in Alushta, not far from his own.

He recalled the small port on the Crimean Peninsula with its nightingales, roses, fishing, and sailing in the Black Sea. He recalled how they hobbled, barefoot, on the steep pebble beach while swimming, how the village retreated up a slope from the sea. Yurii remembered the vineyards, orchards, rose gardens, and houses that decorated those cultivated hills curled up to the sleeping Bear Mountain above the town. He loved those hills and the sea.

Radion Epifanov had lived by the sea. He walked on its beaches. He fished in it. He sailed on it and swam in it. Wrote poetry about it and painted it. Finally, he died in it.

The night of the fourteenth of August was one of the longest Yurii had ever known. He entered the day's events in the ship's log and tried to compose a letter to Radion's parents. He had seen men die. He had lost shipmates, but this was the first man under his command to die. He was charged with their safety, and they trusted him. His agony was almost too great to endure. He wondered if he was fit to command.

On the sixteenth, near Bornholm, the *Neva* fell in with a number of frigates and sloops from different nations. Lisianski was cheered to discover that she was sea kindly, even with her bluff bows and round bottom. That night she lay at anchor alongside her sister ship *Nadezhda* at a place called Stevens on Bornholm Island.

On the seventeenth, both ships sailed into the roads of Copenhagen. The water had soured in the water casks, so the casks were emptied, their interiors were scorched, and a small amount of charcoal was added to each one. Thereafter, the water remained fresh.

Lisianski also learned that confined compartments could be fumigated with a mixture of magnesia negra, common salt, and oil of vitriol. He pumped fresh seawater mixed with burnt lime into the hold twice a week and drained it. The hatches were removed whenever weather permitted. The bilge remained sweet.

During the night of the eighteenth of September, the barometer fell twenty millibars. The crews secured the ships' boats and equipment as the wind backed east of south and hardened. The glass fell another seven millibars. The sky darkened with one squall after another. Pelting white rain sizzled in the dawn light. Visibility reduced to a few feet. Both ships lit running lights. Heavy seas broke over the weather rail, ran down the lee gutter, and cascaded over the starboard poop.

The crew struggled lowering the main and mizzen. Fore and aft sails were eased. Wind howled to a high-pitched scream in the masts and rigging. The seas hissed and water dashed about the deck, drumming against the superstructure.

Hatches were secured, but leaks and condensation dampened clothing and racks in the close atmosphere below decks. After a roaring twenty hours, the storm subsided, easing into a sunlight-following breeze.

It became clear that the *Neva* sailed closer to the wind than the frigate *Nadezhda*, even though the frigate was a much bigger ship. A wonderful coalescence of length along the water, sail plan, skillful navigation, and good crew rendered the Baltic collier, converted to war sloop, a stout and true sailor. Lisianski ground his teeth when forced to rein her in to keep pace with the *Nadezhda*, but he knew that such is the case when mismatched vessels and crew sail in convoy.

On the evening of the nineteenth of September, a rosette aurora shimmered until dawn. The ship sailed through the night, cleaving rose petals, as the bell chimed the hours. The binnacle light cast a yellow halo about the bearded face of the helmsman as the aroma of freshly brewed tea drifted up from the galley. The *Neva* was clear of the Cattegut and separated by the storm from the *Nadezhda*. Reefs were shaken out, and she ran free. On the twenty-third, her latitude was 51°58', in sight of the English coast. She made for Dungeness.

From an English frigate, Lisianski learned that the storm had dismasted several other ships and driven some ashore. He was pleased with his stout ship and good crew. They were well suited for the voyage ahead.

The *Neva* dropped anchor at Falmouth on the twenty-fourth. A six-gun salute was exchanged. While they waited for the *Nadezhda*. *Neva*'s decks were caulked and a new suit of sail bent on. The officers and men were given shore leave. It would be the last European port they would enter. After three days, the *Nadezhda* brought-to alongside. Her sides had opened in the storm; she wanted a thorough caulking.

Finally, by the fifth of October, the convoy got under way. They left Lizard Point on a fair wind. On the tenth, a number of exhausted petrels took refuge on the deck, only to be attacked by the ship's cats. The weather remained wet and gloomy until the seventeenth. The time was filled with burning charcoal in the hold, sprinkling warm vinegar in musty cubbies, and scraping the deck. Lisianski preferred scraping to swabbing the deck in such damp weather.

With the approach of the tropics, the air warmed and weather improved. Lisianski ordered winter clothing stowed. He announced that every morning one-third of the crew would, by rotation, turn out and wash themselves from head to foot in seawater. The men grumbled as grog was substituted for brandy.

On the morning of the nineteenth of October, Tenerife was descried, forty-five miles to the southwest. Mount Pic reflected brilliant sunlight above a purple sea. The landfall brought Lisianski faith in his navigation and gratitude to God.

The mast head sang out, "Deck there! Frigate."

"Where away?"

"Dead astern."

"What colors?"

"None."

By evening, the frigate was within range and closing.

"Beat to quarters!"

"Larboard six-pounders, grapeshot!"

"Run 'em out!"

"She shows colors. French privateer."

"Hoist the ensign!"

"Ahoy! What ship is that and whence and whither?" called Captain Lisianski in French.

"*L'Egyptienne*. Out of Le Havre and bound to seek our fortune. What ship is that and whence and whither?"

"The *Neva* in convoy with the *Nadezhda*, out of Kronstadt, on an expedition to Alaska. We are at the command of Tsar Alexander, with safe passage guaranteed by Napoleon."

"We mistook you for an English merchantman."

"Do we look like an English merchant?"

"Not from here. Fare thee well." With that *L'Egyptienne* pulled in her claws, closed her gun ports, and sheered off, bound for mischief.

At daybreak on the twentieth, the *Neva* dropped anchor in the harbor of Santa Cruz de Tenerife. Lisianski recalled that Nelson had lost an arm there in 1797. The town provided excellent water and plenty of livestock, fruits, and vegetables. All were set at a high price, except for the wine. Lisianski purchased fresh provisions and wine. He observed: "The lower class of inhabitants are so poor they sleep under sacks, using the street as a bed-chamber. They subsist on stinking fish."[2] He noted that the mooring ground was strewn with rocks and lost anchors.

On the twenty-seventh of October, the *Neva* departed the Canary Islands. By the twenty-ninth, the air was close and humid. Lisianski's crew had never been beyond the North Sea. He ordered lemon juice added to the grog. Occasionally wine was substituted for the grog and juice. An awning was spread on the deck. All were enjoined not to appear on deck without a cap.

Soon the ship caught the northeast trades, and the crew lazed on deck watching their companions, the grampus, bonito, and dolphin. Lisianski provided the crew with copies of Anson and Cook. Those who could, read to the others as the ship surfed along with a following sea. The crew relished the bounty of flying fish. Hammocks appeared on deck. The men dozed in shaded breezes as they swayed gently to sleep, gazing at the passing clouds. There was, after all, little to do other than stand watch and repair gear. They rested with the rhythms and sounds of following wind and sea.

Lisianski spent hours watching the ever-changing but constant roll of the seas—rising astern, passing under the ship, and rolling on toward the horizon. His mind eased into a hypnotic and tranquil state. The waves rose, approached, and passed, each in its time, to be replaced by another. Each was unique but always the same, a significant event but insignificant in a train of unending events, combining to form the great Atlantic Ocean. Each wave was a bedazzling, beautiful, yet ordinary thing; each was a threat, but a peaceful addition to the continuum of existence, each more or less significant than the

---

2   The majority of Lisianski quotations are from his account of the circumnavigation: *Путешествие вокруг Света на Корабле* Нева *1803–1806.*

other, a part of the whole, combining in a seamless past, present, and future, each filled with change and constancy, providing the illusion that is existence. In such a state, Lisianski's mind, cleared of petty concerns, gave way to the blissful awareness of here and now. Here was nowhere in particular, and now was adrift on an irrelevant sea. The rise and fall of events passed under the keel, and the ship sailed on, homeward bound, to oblivion.

Shaping a southerly course, Lisianski sailed west of the Cape de Verde Islands. He avoided passing through them, aware, from an earlier voyage aboard the English *Raisonnable*, of the dangerous variable winds, calms, and currents that prevail. On the sixteenth of November, the *Neva* sailed out of the northeast trades and into unsettled winds with thunder, lightning, and rain. Thirty casks of rainwater were collected and used for making spruce beer, a foul-tasting drink but one that helped to avoid the dreadful effects of scurvy. Miserable weather continued until latitude 1°34' North and longitude 22°57' West. The southeast trade was obtained. Suddenly the captain yelled, "Make for the *Nadezhda*."

CHAPTER FIVE

The Bear Hunt

Ol' Galweit told of the bear hunt:

"It was early spring. The bear was still asleep. It was that time when families catch halibut and the first salmon. Hemlock and spruce bark are juicy with sap and there are fresh green stalks of wild celery. People collect seaweed and urchin and the herrin' are spawnin' so there's lots a' eggs. Some hunt the bear just comin' out. Others just watch cubs play on the slopes of snow-covered scree.

"Yaskadut, the Bear Slayer, took some young men to hunt sik, the black bear, but they don't talk about it. It's bad luck to say, 'I'm goin' to hunt bear.' You don't say that. The bear may hear you. So you say, 'I'm goin' for a walk.' That's more polite. They rose before raven's call. They bathed in the stream. They didn't say nothin'. Sometimes bears can hear what you think. Some shaman have huge bear spirits. Once a man married a bear. Another time a woman married a bear. Bears learnt our language long ago.

"The women must sit still and not work or eat while the men hunt or they'll bring bad luck. The men don't eat. They wait until the kill. Each man took his kayani. These magical roots and leaves help take the anger of the bear away and make the men shoot straight.

"They knew where a black sow denned. She might even have cubs. It was better to take the young men to hunt the black bear first.

They can't hunt X'uts until they learn. X'uts has a big golden-brown head and dark-brown rump. When he stands, he is twice as tall as a man. He can knock salmon out of a stream as deep as his shoulder. You try that. See if you are quick and strong enough.

"When you hunt X'uts you must take many experienced men and dogs, for X'uts will hunt you. But they were goin' for just a small black bear. They took their saqs, those bows and arrows made of hemlock and red cedar. Yaskadut always took his tsagal. He always hunted with this spear he called 'tooth.' It had a double-edged slate blade as long as a forearm. The shaft was thick as a man's thighbone and as long as a tall man.

"The snow still lay in the shady spots. The air was crisp and dry. They found the den under the roots of a fallen spruce. Yaskadut was surprised to see that it was open. The young hunters spotted two cubs in a tree. They ran for the tree as Yaskadut crouched to read the ground. Among the smaller black bear tracks were huge prints with claw marks as long as a man's fingers. He yelled: 'X'uts!'

"As Yaskadut turned his head, he caught a smell of musk and blood and turned as X'uts raged through the brush. He'd just killed the sow. His blood was up. He charged up the hill toward Yaskadut, who barely managed to plant his spear and yell his death cry. X'uts came on in a frenzy. His great jaws dripped blood and saliva as he snapped, grunted, and snarled, trying to run and claw the air at the same time. Yaskadut didn't even try to move; X'uts' charge would'a taken him to the young men. X'uts batted at the spear as he rose to his hind feet. His weight carried him down upon Yaskadut. Yaskadut guided his spear under the rib cage. The impact drove the spear through the heart of X'uts. He fell upon Yaskadut with a roar that ended in a death rattle.

"The young hunters ran to help. Yaskadut's chest was crushed under a weight equal to that of ten men. His back was broken and ribs pierced his heart. They rolled X'uts off the body. They knew there are worse ways to die.

"The hunters climbed the tree and knocked the cubs to the ground, killin' them as they fell. They found the body of the sow. They skinned X'uts and sewed his hide into a huge bag to carry the meat, fat, and intestines of the black bears. Their meat is sweeter and the gut whiter. They could not carry the meat and Yaskadut, so they cremated him. They took Yaskadut's ashes home to the burial house. A potlatch was giv'n the next summer in his honor They prayed to the bears. askin' forgiveness for killin' 'em.

"They thanked the bear for the tongue and jaws to be used by the shaman for powerful magic, the teeth for pendants and amulets, beads, and tools for smoothin' the weave of water baskets. They explained that the intestines make waterproof jackets with hoods. The bear's gut provides watertight bags and windowpanes for the bathhouses. The bladder is used as a harpoon float. The big leg bones are good for makin' skinnin' tools for weasels and mink. The hunters honored X'uts by singing to him:

"'To the Bear:

"'I am sorry I had to kill thee, Uncle,

"'I had need for thy meat.

"'My children were hungry and cryin' for food.

"'Forgive me, Uncle.

"'I honor thy courage, thy strength.

"'I place thy head on this rock facin' the mountain,

"'I want thee to see thy home.

"'Each time I pass this place, I will remember thee, honorin' thy spirit.

"'I am sorry I had to kill thee.

"'Forgive me, Uncle."

The other boys teased little Yaskadut. They challenged him to fight. They called him "Gaxtan." When he fought, he frequently won, with guile or speed. He was startlingly fierce and quick to inflict pain.

Once, Qa-tla watched three boys surround Yaskadut. One boy slipped behind Yaskadut and got down on all fours. The other two yelled in his face, trying to distract him, but Yaskadut felt the presence of the third. The largest boy in the village, YaK̲wáan, suddenly pushed Yaskadut over the back of the boy on the ground.

Yaskadut instinctively grabbed YaK̲wáan's shirt as he fell backwards. He pulled YaK̲wáan down with him as his legs went up, striking the other boy in the waist. YaK̲wáan flipped over Yaskadut. He landed on the icy ridges footprints had formed in the snow, cutting his face and hands. Yaskadut was amazed that he had thrown YaK̲wáan over his head. The other kids thought he had done it on purpose. They said that he was treacherous. YaK̲wáan sulked and withdrew.

Yaskadut spent most of his time alone. He entered woods that most children feared. He spent entire days deep in the forest, only to return late at night and sleep next to the fire pit with the slaves.

He played in an alder grove. The long, thin limbs branched out low to the ground. He could climb one and ride it down, then grab the next from a nearby tree. As he climbed higher, that limb would descend until it touched its neighbor. In that manner, he could travel the length of the grove without touching the ground. He stripped the layers of bark from birch trees and made small boats. In the spring, puddles, ponds, and streams formed everywhere. He placed his boats in the streams and raced along the banks as they were swept away.

He shot fish with a three-pronged fishing arrow. He learned to shoot below the image of the fish to hit it. He would roast the fish and have a feast. He wandered along the banks of the streams, stepping on dead salmon to squirt roe upon the gravel. Once, while eating currants from a bush, he glanced across a small stream to see a black bear doing the same on the other bank. They ran in opposite directions. Another time, he heard a noise deep in the brush. He quietly circled and discovered YaK̲wáan trying to spy on him. Yaskadut hit YaK̲wáan in the back of the head with a handful of bear shit. Startled, YaK̲wáan ran into the woods, howling like a witch.

He learned early about the devil's club. It had a lush canopy of huge leaves, but beneath, along the stalks, were long, razor-sharp thorns. They cut through clothing and flesh almost unnoticed.

He strolled along the rocky beaches and examined tide pools full of shellfish and sea animals. He played with long strands of sea kelp, cracking them like whips. He stepped on polyps to feel and hear them crunch underfoot. He watched the turnstones, avocets, and godwits play tag with the sea. Gulls and terns wheeled overhead, chattering.

He watched humpbacks roll and the fins of orca knife through the sound. He was fascinated by the constantly changing surf. He examined the rainbow splash of waves crashing upon the rocky shore. The reflections, refraction, color, and shade changes of the sea foam's iridescent bubbles intrigued him.

He sat by tidal pools while bull kelp lapped the feet of coastal rain forests and mink snatched rock crab's legs from the green broth. He wandered into the woods during winter nights along creek banks of alder groves, cottonwoods, and moss-covered spruce that gave

way to white mantled fir, cedar, and pine. When the snow was powder, it spoke to him with a dry, matted voice; when crusty, with a
delicious crunch.

One night the aurora borealis hung in the sky, shimmering
green drapes reflecting off pillows of snow. Even the air was green.
Icicles sparkled emeralds through the still woods. Yaskadut trudged
up a snowy ridge. In a clearing below, a pack of wolves formed a
ring. Two great wolves circled one another in the moonlit center.

Yaskadut stopped dead still. He held his breath until he noticed
that the breeze was in his face. He watched intently as a battle for
dominance reached its frenzy of snarls, fangs, and blood. Suddenly
aware of his peril, he ran, crashing through the knee-deep snow as
he imagined the pack overtaking him and pulling him down.

That night he lay by the fire pit, unable to sleep. He was happy
that he had been allowed to observe the battle of the wolves. He was
learning the secrets of the forest.

He especially liked to climb a mountain beyond the woods
that lay behind the village. He tried to follow game trails or travel
in streambeds to reach the base of the mountain. Often he was com-
pelled to crawl and wriggle through tangles of fallen moss-covered
logs while a springy ten-foot-deep ground cover of matted windfall,
rotting vegetation, lichen, and moss clutched at him. Devil's clubs
cut into his legs until blood mingled with peat moss and wild roses.

He delighted in the sparkle and dance of the stream. He watched
the things it did with and to sticks, stones, and leaves, jumping, bubbling, gurgling, and swirling in its clever silver course. It changed
constantly, yet remained the same as it flowed to the sea.

Resting during his trek up the mountain, he would sit in meadows of brilliant fireweed, listening to the music of water, rocks,
wind, and leaves. He heard the ancient conversations of the forest,

river, and sky. Sometimes he heard a bright bubbling chatter, sometimes a low dirge. At times, in a wild symphony, thunder accompanied howling wind and groaning trees. On still, sunny mornings, he listened to the minuet of steelhead lazing in the shadows of sunlit pools.

In a cold rain, he learned that the rain was not cold, he was; that the forest was, is, and will be as perceived by its momentary guest. He regretted his mortality, knowing that someday he would not see and hear this place or taste its wind and smell its scent. He wondered why he could not remain always a part of the forest, mountains, and streams.

He knew that most bears would avoid contact if given a chance. In dense copses, he whistled or sang to let bears know he was there. He did not hate the bear, especially the black bear. He was extremely wary of the big browns, who were territorial and might attack on sight. He could smell a bear from a long way off. He always sniffed the air as he approached thickets.

The women believed that if they stood still and exposed their breasts, Uncle Bear would be embarrassed and turn away. The children were taught to make noise and keep an eye out for a likely tree to climb: not too big—bears will climb, and not too small—bears will push it down. The trick was to gauge the bear and the tree in good time.

Deep in the forest, he saw snowshoe rabbits, mink, foxes, and squirrels. At the edge of clearings, he saw wolves and black-tailed deer. Near ponds and streams, he quietly watched beaver. In bogs, he met the moose, but neither he nor they went there at sunset. At sunset, the mosquito ruled supreme.

The summer forest floor was adorned with ferns and wild roses. A carpet of moss and decaying vegetation gave with each step. Every tree, bush, and fern held secret caves, rooms, and hideouts. When he was perfectly quiet, he could hear Cedar Man, a giant red cedar, stretch and wriggle his toes in the tangled community of peat moss, fungi, mushrooms, and mold.

The folds of this gigantic red cedar's bark were home to full-grown hemlock trees, azaleas, and huckleberries. Monstrous limbs sported moss, liverworts, lichen, and ferns. The fifty-foot circumference of this ancient red cedar provided shelter and safety to generations of plants and animals.

On Yaskadut's passage up the mountain, he walked from the deep shade of the forest to sloping grassy plains above the tree line. Soon the grass yielded to chutes of scree. He slid back a step for every three forward. After scrabbling up the slate, he reached the stone outcroppings below the summit. Here he saw ptarmigan, bigger and fatter than raven. In winter, they were snow white; in summer, their plumage was speckled rock-brown and gray. They trusted their camouflage. If he did not look directly at them or point at them, he could approach within two or three strides. He approached and suddenly pointed. They burst straight up and circled downslope.

The summit was his favorite place. In the morning, Fog Lady swirled among the rocks. He thrilled as he peered into the fog, waiting for something to appear. Thick silence prevailed. When the sun rose, the fog burned off and he could see the village on Shee Atiká Sound. The sunlight was reassuring. At his back, the summit fell away to a blue glacier that disappeared among endless escarpments of mountain peaks, spines, and valleys filled with crimson bearberry, blue spruce, and golden aspen. He lay on moss sprinkled with campion, pink stars, lichen, and stunted white heather. He toyed with the hundred-year-old woody roots and stems of dwarfed willows that spread among the lichen.

As he listened to the sounds of the village far below, he plucked purple crocus or Arctic poppies near arrays of red, gold, and russet lichen. He heard dogs barking and people chopping wood. He saw people moving from house to house. He knew every person and dog that lived in the village and their habits.

Slowly, as he watched and listened, he merged with the sea, sky, and wind. They were no longer separate but all part of the whole, a surging, changing, shifting, pulsating process. He was not lonely. He felt at home on his mountain roost.

On the descent, he flew along the flat scree, bounding from one sliding stone to another. He had to resist the temptation to go faster and faster or his foot would land on a stone that did not move and he would tumble and cut himself on the sharp rocks. When he hit the grassy slope, he lay down and rolled over and over to the tree line. He began to feel so much pain in his legs from walking downslope that he turned uphill for a few steps to relieve it. He arrived late, as the village slept. He slipped onto a bench next to the fire and slept among the slaves.

On one such trip to the mountain, he lay on his belly with his head over the edge of a grassy bank, looking down into a clear stream. A black-tailed doe grazed on the opposite bank. A woodpecker tapped in the woods. Steelhead swam lazily in a deep pool. Yaskadut could see colored pebbles on the bottom. He watched water bugs skate on the surface. He rolled on his back, snuggling into the moss. It was a warm, clear day. He fell asleep watching the clouds form animals in the blue sky.

*   *   *

Yaskadut startled awake, staring straight into three elaborately decorated faces. They bore labrets in distended lower lips; nose bones and beads hung from pierced ears. Their faces were painted black. The people were naked except for broad-brimmed hats decorated with dentalium shells, sea lion whiskers, and figures painted in blue, black, and red. They were smaller than the Tlingit, with large, round heads.

Yaskadut was taken prisoner by a hunting party of the island people called Koniag.

CHAPTER SIX

Dance of death: a light-air battle of frigates

While passing abeam of the *Nadezhda*, Lisianski hailed, "Ahoy, the *Nadezhda*! Captain Kruzenstern!"

Kruzenstern chafed at sailing less efficiently. He curtly replied to the hail, "Yes!"

"Half an hour ago I took a fix at ten minutes south. We are crossing the equator. Congratulations, sir. Three cheers for Fleet Commander Kruzenstern."

"Hurrah! Hurrah! Hurrah!" the crews yelled.

The ships reefed sail and drifted, not more than thirty yards apart. Kruzenstern announced, "We are the first Russian ships to cross the equator. A Russian fleet that plies the seas of the world was a dream that began with Peter the Great. We are the beginning of that dream. Some day the imperial ensign will be seen in every port of the world."

Yurii stood on the quarterdeck in reverie, gazing across the water at Kruzenstern. They had been selected from the top sixteen officers of the fleet and sent to England to complete their naval education; both had been assigned in London to ships in His Majesty's Britannic Navy, where they trained for five years.

Yurii recalled his first assignment on board the frigate *L'Oiseau*. She sailed with a squadron to the east coast of North America. He thought of the capture of a large fleet of American ships and an action against a French ship that tried to run the English blockade of the United States.

He remembered cruiser duty off the coast of Halifax. During a blow in 1795, the *L'Oiseau* sprung a leak and was driven downwind to the West Indies. He had written letters deploring the abuse of the natives of the region: "They were used as one uses wild horses."

He recalled travels to New York and the Eastern Seaboard, where he met George Washington in Philadelphia. He rubbed the scar in his hairline, a memento of a head wound he received while serving on the English frigate *Topaz* during the capture of a French frigate, the *Elizavetta*.

Lisianski ticked off the names of English ships on which he served while visiting Madras and Bombay. He smiled, recalling his promotion to master and commander and his sail aboard the *Raisonnable*, a ship-of-the-line, round the Cape of Good Hope. He savored his return to Russia in 1799 as a captain-lieutenant after seven years of service in the English fleet and smiled at the thought of his command of the frigate *Avtrop* at the age of twenty-four. He touched his medal, the Order of St. George, Fourth Class, given for heroic action during combat in eighteen sea campaigns.

On this occasion, he wore doeskin trousers and a blue, stiff-collar jacket with the gold epaulettes of his rank. His chest was decorated with the St. Vladimir and St. George medals. A white-plumed cockade adorned his tricorner hat. Black knee boots and a saber completed the dress uniform he wore to celebrate the first crossing of the equator by a Russian ship.

He recalled the village of Nezhin in the Ukraine, where he was born on August 2, 1773, the son of an archpriest. His stature and green eyes revealed Viking ancestry, but his dark curly hair and olive skin reflected the Tartar blood of his mother. The unusual combination produced an extremely handsome young man, popular with the ladies. He recognized his pride and vanity.

He remembered standing on the granite shore of Kronstadt, a boy of ten, replete in a marine academy uniform: black leather sea boots, snow-white trousers, and dark-green kurtka with brass buttons and gold epaulettes, topped by a Napoleon hat and armed with a short sword. He had reveled in the study of military maneuvers, sea battles, and distant voyages. He enjoyed the uniforms and disdained the thought of spending his life as a merchant grubbing for profit or a landowner working peasants to death.

Memories of his graduation day came rushing back:

"Yurii Fedorovich Lisianski has acquitted himself well. He is first in his class, receiving only fives. He was outstanding in navigation and seamanship. He is, above all, a gentleman," said Admiral Vorontsev, the commandant of the Cadet Corps.

«Ура! Ура! Мы успели! Закончили!» (Hurrah! Hurrah! We succeeded. We finished!) the cadets yelled, throwing their hats into the air.

«Да Вы хорошо закончили кадеты! Поздравляю Вас!» (Yes, you have finished well, cadets! Congratulations!) "I wish you success, but you will not be free for long. Your assignments are posted."

They all ran to the bulletin board. Yurii searched for notice of his orders:

Лисянский, Юрий Фёдорович В Балт. Флоте под командой Адмирала Грега на борту Фрегит *Подражислав*.

"Yurochka, thou hast a frigate in the Baltic Fleet. The *Podrazhislav*!" shouted a classmate with both pleasure and envy.

"And thee? What is thine?" Yurii asked.

"Nothing special; supply ship," his friend replied with a falling voice and lowered eyes.

"Yurochka, be careful. We are at war with the Swedes."

"I know, I know. Isn't it perfectly wonderful?"

The memory of his baptism of fire swirled in his head.

"Deck there. Frigate!" shouted Midshipman Lisianski.

"Where away?"

"Two points off larboard bow."

"Colors?"

"Swede."

"She's pinned against a lee shore. We'll go about on to the port tack for the wind-gage. Port tack," the captain ordered.

The officer of the deck yelled the commands at the appropriate moment.

"Helm down."

"Aye. Helm down," echoed the watch commander.

"Ease the jib and staysail sheets!"

"Ease jib and staysails."

"Brace up the yards on the foremast!"

"Brace foremast yards."

The foremast main and top swung square to the wind and were back-winded. The ship started to swing to port tack.

"Let her swing, let her swing. Now! Haul in larboard jib! Larboard staysail sheets, haul! Haul!"

The wind caught the leach of the mainsail and the officer of the deck yelled, "Main yards! Lay aholt of those lee main braces! Smart now—haul round the mizzen yards. Let go and haul!"

The drums rolled. Gun crews ran to their batteries. Midshipmen checked rammers, sponges, and powder horns.

Orders rang out:

"Lower battery—double shot!"

"Upper—langrage."

The powder monkeys scurried for shot and powder.

"Cast loose your guns!"

Muzzle lashings were removed and coiled, breach lashings secured.

"Level your guns!"

"Take out tompions!"

"Load cartridge!"

"Shot your guns!"

"Run out!"

The tackle falls that took up recoil were neatly faked on deck. The gun crews stood by as the ships closed.

"Prime!"

The touchhole was primed with gunpowder. The gunner, holding the lighted slow-match, waited for the order.

"Point your guns!"

The gunner kneeled and blew on the match while the crews elevated and adjusted the guns. The gunners waited for the roll of the ship to bring the top sights up to the target.

"Fire!"

It was a minuet, a pas de deux, a dance of death—a light-air battle of frigates. It was ordered chaos as the ships maneuvered and the crews manned the guns.

"Observe her helm and sails. Sing out her every move!"

"She wears to larboard."

"Wear ship!"

"She comes about to starboard."

"Come about!"

"She sets t'gallants."

"Set t'gallants!"

Two great reflected swans shadowed, came about, wore, quartered, and ran, seeking the wind-gage for a rolling broadside up the stern or down the stem of the enemy. Contact was maintained but at maximum range.

The wind shifted. The *Podrazhislav* wore. The Swede wore.

An offshore puffed a head wind; steer full and bye. Wear round and brace the yards. Like two great butterflies, they danced, slowly closing for a deadly embrace.

An onshore breeze drove the *Podrazhislav* down upon the Swede. The Swede fell off, wore about, and fired a port broadside. Smoke. Thunder. The whistle of cannonballs.

"Short! The shot falls short!"

"Helm's alee! Steady! Steady! Fire on the rise. Fire! Fire! Come about! Hold! Hold! On the rise … Fire at will!"

The ship heeled violently. Yurii's perch on the main masthead traveled through fifteen degrees of arc. The shots bracketed the Swede, blew up a gun port, and toppled the mizzen royal. The Swede gained ground toward a spit that defined her embayment. The *Podrazhislav* staggered but caught the wind abeam and pursued the Swede. The gun crews sponged the guns, rammed home the powder cartridge and shot, primed, and touched off the cannon with portfires.

Blood, smoke, splintered wood, and shot raged in Yurii's head. His throat was dry, his voice cracked. His thoughts raced in confusion. He yelled, screamed, laughed, and cried. His detached hands, arms, and legs did practiced things. Surreal events occurred in slow motion. He was isolated, above the scene of crimson bodies and blood gushing through the scuppers of the ships.

The Swede laid the mark round the spit. She caught an eddying offshore puff, just as the *Podrazhislav* lost her onshore breeze and drifted into confused winds. The breeze and current carried the Swede beyond range toward the horizon.

"Hurrah!" The crew exploded with victory and relief. Pursuit was vain, as the *Podrazhislav* drifted into the wind shadow of the landmass. Yurii's relief came on, and he descended to the deck.

"Well, Yurii Andreevich, what did you learn?" asked the captain.

"It was difficult even to think, but we are better sailors and fighters than the Swedes."

"Battle is no time to think; you must act. We closed too soon. We should have sailed for the headland. Next time, the wind may favor them."

Yurii's musing was interrupted when a bumper of Tenerife was served round and a great celebration of the crossing of the equator began. Neptune appeared with trident and crown of seaweed. The crews regaled themselves with brandy and wine. They feasted on duck, potatoes, and plum pudding washed down with one bottle of port for every three men, and gallons of Tenerife wine. All the guns of both ships were fired. Both captains forbade the custom of throwing initiates overboard, since that included the entire crew. Laughter, tears, toasts, and cheers continued into the evening.

Yurii shared his thoughts with Arbuzov. "It is heady wine to capture the wind and navigate the stars. It is the gift of freedom. It is recompense for knowledge hard won. A good ship and a skillful crew can take you to paradise. Those who dare disdain the shore-bound!"

By nightfall on November 26, 1803, everyone on board both ships was perfectly drunk.

*   *   *

Lisianski considered sea currents vital information. He kept meticulous charts to aid in future navigation. He worked to prepare the way for Russia's commerce with nations.

As the ship approached the coast of Brazil, he took precautions to protect the men from unscrupulous Brazilians. He knew from experience that they encouraged sailors to get drunk and sell all their clothes and personal belongings. He forbade individual trading, placing the men's gear and personal property under the charge of the petty officers.

On the eleventh of December, the ship was engulfed in a cloud of butterflies. The lead revealed a bottom of shells, coral, and pebbles at a depth of fifty-five fathoms. Cape Frio appeared. Dorado escorted the ships over the Tropic of Capricorn. The Cape's known location was used to check the ship's chronometers and compass variation.

Foreman Terenshii Neklyudov trailed a line baited with a white feather off the stern. A four-foot dorado hit. The fish leapt into the air, shaking its head to throw the hook. It sped ahead of the ship, trying to overtake the line; it swam from side to side under the ship, trying to foul the line. It dove and leapt into the air, rolling and twisting. It flopped over the waves, shaking the hook in midair. It lay on its side and played dead or merely rested as it was pulled to the ship. When a net was lowered, it jumped, jerked the line, shook its head, and tumbled wildly—all in vain.

Stretched out on the deck, the fish passed through a rainbow of iridescent colors, from bright canary yellow to parrot green, then dull gray as it died. Its flesh was firm and clean. The taste was so delicate that a slice of lemon would permeate an entire fillet. Dorado was a welcome change to the ship's diet.

The *Neva* coasted seven miles off the shore of Brazil, seeking the Island of St. Catherine. The weather became too hazy for a meridian altitude.

On the eighteenth of December, clouds gathered and thunder rolled to the south. The ship lay becalmed. Sail was quickly shortened as a heavy rainsquall came on. All sails were brailed except foresail and mizzen-topsl'. It grew dark. The wind blew and the seas ran extremely high.

Seeing the *Nadezhda* approach, Lisianski ordered the foresail brailed and the wind kept near. *Nadezhda* hoisted her fore-top-mast staysail and bore away at the point of collision. After forty-eight hours of rough sailing, the ships found themselves back where they had started.

At length, the Island of Alverado appeared and a pilot came aboard. The *Neva* remained in the offing until sunrise. By noon, she dropped anchor off the Isle of St. Catherine. Portuguese flags were hoisted above the castle and an officer boarded.

Rot was discovered in the main and foremasts of the *Neva*. Replacements were needed. The next seven days were filled with harvesting red olio. The trunks of these trees were straight and tall enough to provide masts without joints for a first-rate man-of-war. The old masts were fir. The new masts were not as light and pliable, but they were much stronger. They were also heavier. As a consequence, Lisianski ordered them shortened by four feet. They served excellently. The *Neva* still sat on her waterline as before, and there was no significant loss of speed.

As a result of the delay for repairs, Lisianski had time to travel the island and note down her charms. "The luxuriant verdure and rich fertility, which this favored isle presents to the view, form a singular contrast with the surrounding elements," he wrote. "Observing everywhere on the shore, woods of orange and lemon-trees; hills crowned with fruit-trees; valleys, plains, and fields interspersed with odoriferous plants, and beautiful flowers, which seem to spring up almost spontaneously; the eye becomes enchanted with the prospect.

"The air is soft and fresh, and while the smell is delighted with the perfumes that balm it, the ear, in silent rapture, listens to the warbling of numerous birds, which seem to have selected this beautiful spot for their habitation. The senses, in short, are all gratified; everything we see, hear, or feel, opens the heart to the sweetest sensations. These charming shores might be called Nature's own paradise; for so lavish had she been of her bounties, that she has favoured them with an eternal spring."

The island proved a pleasant place to spend Christmas and New Year's. Lisianski noted the population was made up of Europeans, "Native Americans," and Negroes.

He wrote, "The condition of the later, unfortunate race in this island, is less wretched than of their brethren in the West Indies, or in any European colony that I have yet visited. Nearly the whole of them have been converted to Christianity by their Portuguese masters, and they have already a black St. Benedict to apply to, in case of emergency. The native Americans here are so shy that no intercourse takes place between them and the Portuguese; I therefore saw very little of them. The governor told me that they mistake the Negroes for monkeys, and kill them, whenever they meet them alone. It seems hardly credible that human beings should exist so lost of reason, as not to distinguish a creature of their own species from brutes; and I cannot help regarding the account as a story purposely fabricated to keep the slaves from running away."

Lisianski documented an abundance of inexpensive supplies such as excellent water, plenty of European and Indian corn, sugar, coffee, rum, pigs, bullock, fowl, duck, fresh vegetables, and fruit. He sketched and noted the locations of forts and the number and placement of guns and troops.

He was delighted with the "wonderful little insect," the firefly. He was so fascinated with their light that several times he had swarms of them placed in a glass container. He then sat and read by the light they generated.

The ships departed St. Catherine on February 4, 1804. For seven glorious days the seas sluiced by the freeboard. Taut braces moaned and the rigging hissed as salt spray slapped athwart the bow. The *Neva* and the *Nadezhda* bowled along on green rollers down the coast of South America. Full and by they sailed into the southerlies, racing now in tandem, now abeam, toward the bottom of the earth and frozen seas.

In the midst of this steady breeze and exhilaration, Captain Lisianski turned dour and agitated. He ordered preparations for bad weather. New seizings were applied, halyards replaced, and lashings tightened. The decks were cleared. Storm sails were laid out, strengthened, and restitched.

The weather held until the brown water of Rio de la Plata lapped the starboard bow. Suddenly, thunderclouds appeared, along with a bite in the air. There was a smell of excitement and fear on board.

Midshipman Kavedyaev's sleepy watch was interrupted by green light emanating from the sea. He rubbed his eyes, staring into the darkness. It looked like the luminous flash of surf where there should be no rocks. He had seen the chart and the projected line of sail. He sounded the alarm.

"Shoals! Dead ahead!"

CHAPTER SEVEN

Capture and Arctic Drift

The raiding party traveled day and night, north by northwest, along the coast. Yaskadut was bound, gagged, and stowed in the bottom of a baidar. The baidar was a boat built on a frame consisting of stem, gunwales, thwarts, ribs, keelson, and side laths. It was covered with walrus hides. There were seventeen men in the boat, a steersman and eight paddlers on each side. After five days of hard paddling, they arrived at their village.

Yaskadut was forced to gather wood and fetch water. They watched him constantly but did not greatly abuse him. In time, he learned their language. They were keen fishermen, using spears, nets, weirs, hooks, and line. Much of their food was gathered from tidelands. They had a saying: "When the tide goes out, the table is set." They timed their days and nights by the sea.

They hunted seal, sea lion, and sea otter from their baidari. On occasion, they hunted the great whale with toggle-headed harpoons attached to sealskin floats.

Eventually, Yaskadut was allowed to go along on these hunts, but only as a paddler and bailer. He was not allowed to use weapons. The Koniag called him "hawk baby" because of his piercing eyes, sharp nose, and small size.

The Koniag traded with people that Europeans called "Eskimos," from Chugach. After two years with the Koniag, Yaskadut was traded to their neighbors from the Chugach region.

Years later, Yaskadut learned of the fate of the Koniag. The Russian hunters and traders, called Promishliniki, came. Before long, the young men were enticed or forced to join the hunt for furs. The women, left alone, were soon cleaning fish, sewing parkas, picking berries, and digging roots for the Promishliniki instead of for their own families.

Although there were only a few Russians, their muskets and steel had a profound effect. The children and old men were forced to collect more bird eggs than usual, as the Promishliniki hoarded everything else edible. These invaders kept all of the furs and hides, so native clothing had to be fashioned out of bird skins. Murder, disease, and assimilation decimated the Koniag.

The Chugach of Pulagvik wore outer garments that reached to their knees, made of seal, fox, raccoon, marten, and sea otter pelts. They also had great coats of depilated caribou hide, cut open at the sides below the armpits. The caribou hides were obtained from trade with "Stick People" from the interior. Eagle, cormorant, and guillemot skins were used for raincoats that reached to the ankles.

In cold weather, the men donned suits made of black bear hide. The head was fashioned into a hood, and the legs were used as sleeves, mittens, trousers, and boots. High-topped boots were made of sea lion pelts; an insole of grass, moss, or a swatch of mountain goat fleece provided warmth. The whole boot laced up the front. The entire leg of the brown bear, including feet and claws, provided hip boots. Conical hats of woven spruce roots, decorated with painted designs, dentalia shells, and sea lion whiskers, were worn in the frequent rain. Undergarments were aprons made of the skin of newborn seals, tied with a string around the neck and waist. They were decorated with beads and fringes.

The Chugach wore labrets, nose bones, and ear ornaments. They also wore beaded headbands. At feasts, they donned feathers dyed with cranberry and blueberry juice. On special occasions, they painted their faces red, blue, gray, and black. One Chugach told Yaskadut that they painted their faces black when going to war so that the enemy could not see them turn pale with fear.

Yaskadut did not know how old he was or how long he had been with the Chugach. They, like the Tlingit, reckoned years by seasons but kept no count of them. The age of a man did not matter. What he had done and what he was capable of doing was significant. Hunting trips and wars, not years, brought honor. Breath and blood mattered, not past and future. No one ever said, "He was a great warrior." If a man became a great warrior, he remained a great warrior. Old age and frailty did not diminish the spirit, the memory, or the honor.

Tides set the time of day, mean high high and mean low low, spring and neap. The currents, flood, slack, and ebb, determined when and where one traveled. Distance was not a linear measurement; the distance to a place was measured by the tide changes before arrival. The only possible mode of travel was by boat.

The Chugach occupied Prince William Sound. Spruce, hemlock, and yellow cedar grew in abundance. Along the beaches were alder, willow, and cottonwood. The interior consisted of steep, impenetrable slopes, barred by great rocks and tangled windfall. Moss, swamps, skunk cabbage, and huckleberry brambles covered the lowlands.

In and around the few open spaces grew salmonberries, cloudberries, blueberries, strawberries, sweet hemlock bark, cow parsnips, nettles, and devil's clubs. In the summer, blue stork's bill, pink columbine, fragrant meadow sweet, yellow cinquefoil, and snapdragons bloomed. Toward fall, clouds of fireweed blazed in the meadows.

On the sandy spits of islands were rye grass, sandwort, beach pea, and strawberry. The Chugach collected black seaweed and ribbon seaweed, cockles, clams, and crabs from the rocky beaches.

There were great numbers of mountain goats, moose, black and brown bear, ground squirrels, woodchuck, fox, wolves, lynx, marten, weasel, mink, land otter, beaver, and muskrat.

The meadows and mountains were filled with wood grouse, ptarmigan, hummingbirds, raven, stellar jays, sparrows, pipits, and redpolls.

Cormorants, kittiwake, gulls, albatross, pigeon guillemot, oyster catchers, puffins, sea parrots, and sandpipers provided eggs, feathers, skins, and bones. The call of the red-throated loon could be heard. The bald eagle feasted on salmon. Sandhill cranes entertained with their courtship dances. Brent geese and great flocks of ducks provided food and clothing.

Yaskadut and the Chugach caught the king, red, humpback, dog, and silver salmon. Steelhead, Dolly Varden, halibut, herring, oelachen, and octopus were taken.

Especially important to the Chugach were the finwhales, humpback, porpoise, white whale, and the feared orca gladiator. They hunted fur seal, spotted seal, sea lion, and sea otter. At the sealing camps in June and July, the men hunted while the women flensed the carcasses, dried the meat, rendered the fat, and stretched the skins.

When the sea would not permit fishing, they gathered barnacles, mussels, limpets, whelks, clams, cockles, chitons, and sea urchin. There was no hunger.

Kuimariaq, a qayaq maker, finally took in Yaskadut. He was a vigorous old man fond of hunting and fishing. He had no family. Yaskadut was diligent and quick, and the old man liked him. He taught the boy how to build qayaqs.

The frame of the Chugach qayaq was made of hemlock, while the stem, stern, and cross pieces were spruce. The entire qayaq was lashed together with spruce root. The Chugach, unlike the Inuit to the north, had abundant woods.

The qayaq, most commonly used for hunting, was the two-hatch variety. Thwart straps were placed in front of each hatch to secure weapons. A harpoon and a bow were carried forward on the port side, a throwing board and a seal club were stowed on the starboard side, and a lance was carried just before the aft hatch on the port side, along with a second bow and a wooden arrow quiver. A whaling lance was also carried on the port side of the aft hatch. A spindle-shaped siphon made of two halves of hollowed-out wood, lightly lashed together, allowed the bailer to suck up water by placing his finger over a hole and dumping it overboard. Chugach paddles were made with a single blade.

When Kuimariaq made a qayaq, he measured the pieces against his body. The length of the stem piece to the first hatch was one arm-span. The diameter of the hatches was one forearm plus the length of one hand. The length of the gunwale was three arm-spans plus one forearm and hand and yet another hand with outstretched fingers. The beam amidships was one arm and hand.

Kuimariaq, Yaskadut, and seven others took an umiak to hunt fur seals. Umiaks were large, open hunting boats covered with walrus or sea lion hide. The seals migrated north in spring, and the men paddled close ashore toward the northwest. They intended to make their kill out to sea and return with a following southerly swell and current.

The wind came up as they spotted a small herd of walrus on a decaying ice floe. A storm system had carried the Pribilof walrus south from the Bering into the North Pacific. It was unusual to find walrus this far south. The hunters paddled to the far side of the melting floe and pulled the umiak onto the ice, then crept on their bellies toward the walrus. Just as they sprang to the attack, the ice floe shifted, washing the umiak off the ice. They raced for it, but it drifted in the current and caught the wind. The walrus lumbered off the floe. The hunters had no food or fire.

The winds from the storm backed to the southeast. Wind and spray chilled the huddled party as they waited to drift south. Instead, they were carried north, and the wind pushed them out to sea. After twenty days on the ice, the weakest started to die. The survivors stripped the dead and stacked the bodies to form a windbreak. The clothes of the dead were used for cover. Kuimariaq cut pieces of flesh from the bodies. He forced the others to eat, but they grew weak. They died one by one. On the evening of the twenty-eighth day, Kuimariaq began singing his death poem. He sang of hunts, wars, mountains, and seas. He whistled to bring the northern lights closer. They were the souls of fallen hunters and warriors that he wished to join. He spoke to Imam-fua, the spirit ruler of the oceans, who lived in the deep, ruling over the sea animals. He asked her to take Yaskadut home to Shee Atiká.

Kuimariaq gave Yaskadut permission to make use of his body: "Yaskadut, when I die, add my body to the windbreak." He laughed as he observed that his old flesh would not be juicy. He died.

Yaskadut floated northwest along the great Aleutian Island Chain. He drifted in a saline desert on a salt-rimed sea. Rain seldom fell. Herds of bowhead migrated through the leads with their traveling companions, the beluga. Heedless, sea ducks flew overhead. Closer ashore lay stacked ice in an impossible maze of pearl white and dove gray. Milky-blue water accented cracks and fissures. Edges of floes reflected the marine-blue sea.

At twilight, pale shades of pink, rose, and yellow contrasted with a violet ocean. Sun and moon halos, rings, and coronas hazed through ice-filled refracting clouds. The aurora borealis appeared, a pale, undulating drape.

Yaskadut grew cold. He placed his hands on his stomach for warmth. He sat still to preserve energy. Snow collected around his bundled body. He chewed on frozen pieces of flesh and sucked icicles hanging from the grisly windbreak. As he drifted and the wind howled, he became drowsy. He no longer felt cold. His hands and feet did not sting or ache. Drowsiness caressed him. He dreamt of a young woman's warmth under the furs of home. Sleep lay with him.

CHAPTER EIGHT

The Horn. All hands on Deck!

"Helm alee!" yelled Lieutenant Arbuzov, the watch officer. "All hands on deck!"

The decks flooded with men. From the quarterdeck, Captain Lisianski saw the humpback whale, mistaken for shoals. Just below the water's surface, it glowed an eerie green. The whale silently drifted the length of the ship in the starlit night. A massive eye rolled above the water, majestically indifferent to the officers and crew. They stared at the spectacle of the whale, detailed in the luminescence of its passing. All stood quietly, peering into another world, an alien montage of light, sound, and motion that thrived, multiplied, and died, completely oblivious to and independent of man, living on a separate scale, with a distinct rhythm and raison d'être.

The ship's surgeon, Morits Liband, was fascinated by the green light. He and several men remained on deck observing the florescence of the bow and stern wakes. They noted the darts of light left by excited fish. They saw dolphins streak by, glowing like meteors in a velvet sky.

"Captain, what causes the water to glow when disturbed?"

"I don't know. I have seen this effect before but do not know its cause. The motion of the ship through the water excites it."

Lisianski liked this surgeon, who played Mozart on his violin. He was a rare catch. Unlike most of the ships' surgeons, he was neither a drunk nor an incompetent. He was a well-educated, skillful surgeon. He came aboard out of a mixture of scientific curiosity and midlife ennui.

The captain and the surgeon worked well together. They had conferred at length in mixing up various antiscorbutic concoctions that the crew thoroughly disliked. One of the most hated was the essence of malt dissolved in hot water with a dose of cod liver oil.

The two men became so curious about the glowing sea that they conducted several experiments. In the half-light of morning, they caught some seawater in sailcloth. They noticed that spots on the cloth sparkled and concluded that it was caused by some organism. They doubled a fine cloth over a dish and poured seawater over it. Several spots remained on the cloth that glistened when the cloth was shaken.

"I think it is phosphorous," Liband concluded.

"Let's add some sawdust in the water and see if the phosphorous clings."

There was no residue of phosphorous on the sawdust. They examined the water under a microscope and discovered "animalculae" in the shape of tiny crabs and fibers, and concluded that these tiny crustaceans, like the fireflies of St. Catherine's Island, generated their own light when agitated.

As they sailed down the Patagonian coast through the roaring forties, it grew colder. The temperature fell and warm clothes were broken out. Pumpkins and onions were boiled with salted meat. Generous amounts of pea soup were provided.

Lisianski, in the tradition of his naval training, understated the winds and seas in his log as "fine breezes, somewhat squally" or "fresh gales with westerly swell." On one occasion, he even entered "heavy seas," describing seas that washed the brow overboard, obliging them to shorten to staysails. Cold, rain, winds, heavy seas, and hail assaulted them. On occasion, the hail was so fierce that no one could face it while on deck.

On the eighteenth and nineteenth of March, calm weather prevailed. The damp bedding and stinking clothes were aired. The course was almost due south to $58°$ 30' latitude, then east along that latitude to $80°$ longitude. From that point, they planned to sail due north. The course was intended to avoid the southwest winds and the westerly swell that frequent the Cape. In late April, Lisianski made a brief entry in the ship's log—his last for several weeks.

Date: March 24, 1804

Time: 06:00

Lat.: 35° 31' South

Long.: 20° 00' East

Course: 270° degrees, speed 7 knots

Comments: —

But his comments were left unwritten.

"All hands on deck! All hands on deck!"

A drum beats assembly. Cargo and gear shift as the ship heels. Thuds of bare feet on wooden decks mingle with shouts. Wind shrieks through the rigging as hail pelts the deck. Lightning flashes reveal a veer working cross-seas, abetted by an enormous breaking swell. Waves poop the stern, cascading water sweeps the deck. Horizontal flurry slashes numb faces. A maelstrom of graybeards drive down upon the ship. Confused waves collide, bursting straight up, to toss the *Neva* with explosive force.

The fore t'gallant mast snaps and settles, tumbling over the lee rail to trail the weather sheet and t'gallant in the sea. The vagrant sail fills with water, pulling the *Neva* down by the bow. She yaws and heads up, only to fall abeam of the weather. She rolls and shudders with the blows as the seas break over her beams.

A wayward jib sheet whips the leg of a sailor, snatching him overboard. Shreds of sail crack and pop. Hands claw at lines and sail as her upper and lower t'gans'ls, spanker, mainsail, crojik, jigger stays'ls, and jibs are struck. She flies a hazardly brailed mizzen but plunges through the wave crest and drops into a trough of black water. The helmsman lies in the leeward scuppers with a shattered forearm.

Captain Lisianski races across the listing deck to the helm. Wind stifles his shouted orders. As he struggles to force the helm amidships, the *Neva* heels to starboard. She broaches and is knocked on her beam-ends for a full three minutes before slowly righting through green water.

She skids, catches her footing, and surfs to the bottom of a trough, shuddering, stalling, and staggering as she rises, dumping the onboard sea. The following seas mount in stages of steep and gradual slopes, forming a complex of peaks and mountain meadows.

The *Neva* climbs, catches the wind, surges forward, tops a wave, and plunges through the crest, then falls, keel flat, fifty feet into the bottom of the next trough. Rigging showers down upon the deck. Lisianski visualizes the masts driven through the keel.

The helm jams hard over. The sea springs the rudder-fit pintles in the gudgeon. The tackle of a 1,700-pound iron carronade explodes; the gun, on elm wood wheels, rumbles across the deck, shattering the lee rail. The 370-ton war sloop is tossed like a skiff. Each time she rises, Lisianski experiences relief. Each sea is a threat that mounts, is accommodated, and falls away, only to begin again.

Yurii feels the sea loom as a concave wall of following water breaks upon the stern. He pitches headfirst into the helm as the water crushes his chest, gasping for air as the green sea rolls over him. Blood gushes into his eyes. Nausea drains his consciousness. He instinctively wraps around the binnacle.

Another breaker rolls over him. The shrieking seas speaks:

"Death has no finality."

He gasps for air as eddies swirl about his body.

"Death is but a process of life."

The water chuckles and tugs at his limbs, beckoning.

"Death is the innate consequence of life."

Another comber sweeps aboard. A dark whirlpool lifts him off the deck.

"Death gains definition by the particular."

His body sloshes to and fro. The waves roll on.

"The beginning is the ending, is the beginning, is the ending … is …"

*   *   *

On the twelfth of April, 1804, Lisianski, having recovered, obtained a fix at 51°33' South, 93°29' West. They had rounded the Horn, east to west, from the Atlantic to the Pacific. The ships had become separated. The *Neva* doubled back, but stopped short of sailing back round the Horn. She drifted and sailed in search patterns of ever-greater triangles, firing her cannon and hailing. In the dense fog, blue lights were hoisted. She sailed, stopped, fired her cannon, and listened, then moved on a short distance and repeated the process in accordance with their prearranged signal system. All through the night and into the dawn she searched. Finally, at noon, Lisianski resolved to press on.

The projected line of sail was northwest across the great expanse of the Pacific to Easter Island, across the Tropic of Capricorn to the Marquises, across the equator, on to the Sandwich Islands, and finally, to Kodiak Island, off the coast of Alaska.

They were now alone in the greatest ocean in the world. Immense distances separated them from any hope of rescue. There would be no help. They would sail in waters unknown to them. They would make difficult landfalls on strange islands appearing on charts as mere pinpoints in approximate positions. A missed landfall could mean death. They would survive or perish based on their resources. They were alone at sea without the reassurance of others. It was a daunting prospect and a breathtaking challenge. Exhilaration and fear combined to produce that peculiar sensation called "thrill."

Near Easter Island, at latitude $29^{\circ}45'$ and longitude 104° ' Lisianski had the forge brought on deck to manufacture axes, knives, large nails, and chisels for trade with the South Sea Islanders.

Gray gulls gave away the land. On April 16, 1804, an island came into view. Cables were bent to the anchors. Finding heavy surge with an onshore wind, Lisianski decided not to enter the anchorage at Cook's Bay. Lieutenant Povalishin entered the bay in the jolly boat with knives, small pieces of iron, empty bottles, and some printed linens. He returned in the afternoon with some plantains, bananas, sweet potatoes, yams, and sugarcane. He left a letter for Captain Kruzenstern in a sealed bottle. Lisianski tarried for some five days, surveying the shoreline and waiting for Kruzenstern. At last, he sailed away from the remote island with its monumental and enigmatic stone heads.

On the thirtieth, a northeaster sprang up and carried the *Neva* toward the Marquises. The uneventful sail provided much-needed

rest after the storm they had endured at the Horn. Bonito and tropi-
cal birds escorted the ship.

It was Easter Sunday, and the crew sang, danced, shared bottles of Tenerife, and regaled each other with stories of home in antic-
ipation of landfall. The next two days were spent in surveying the
coasts of the islands. The nights passed hove-to. Lisianski would
not risk a nighttime landfall on an unfamiliar island skirted by coral
reefs. At length, the *Neva* approached the shore at Nukahiva.

At first dawn, a canoe with eight persons made for the anchored
ship. A short distance out, the canoe stopped, and a man blew hard on
a conch and waved a white piece of cloth. The *Neva* waved a white
flag in response and threw a line over the side. The man scrambled
aboard in a friendly and relaxed manner.

Yurii ordered Seaman Zelenin, the quartermaster, to disburse
gifts. The natives were especially pleased with the knives. They
began singing and dancing in delight. Four more canoes approached.
Lisianski indicated that he wanted those he had allowed on board to
leave, and they promptly dove into the sea.

A chief arrived in a canoe, holding a long stick with a bunch
of bananas, a piece of white cloth, and a square fan. Yurii beckoned, and the chief jumped into the water, swam over, and scrabbled
aboard. He gave Yurii the bananas and white cloth. In return, Yurii
placed a cap on his head, but the chief refused it and indicated he
wanted a knife. He was given a knife, earrings made of kopecks, and
a small looking glass. He was so pleased with the looking glass that
he almost lost his senses. Yurii showed the chief and his entourage
pigs, fowls, sheep, and goats. They were extremely curious about
the sheep and goats.

Much to their surprise, the crew of the *Neva* saw the jolly boat
of the *Nadezhda* rowing toward them. Amid shouts of pleasure and

greetings, they learned that the *Nadezhda* had just arrived. She was anchored nearby in the Bay of Taiohae.

Lisianski found the king of the bay and a number of naked islanders on board the *Nadezhda* as he came aboard to pay his respects to Captain Kruzenstern. The king took an instant liking to Lisianski and promised to pay the *Neva* a visit.

An "explanation," in the Russian sense of the word, ensued between Lisianski and Kruzenstern. Being unsure of his reception, Lisianski addressed Kruzenstern formally.

"Captain Kruzenstern, I am greatly relieved and pleased to see you."

"Thank you, Captain Lisianski. I am relieved to find the *Neva* here. It has been seven weeks since we were separated. How fares the ship and crew?"

"We lost one man, another was injured, and the rigging suffered. How fared the *Nadezhda*?"

"Fine. We lost only three seamen and suffered some slight damage to the rigging. It seems we should improve our method of maintaining contact when sailing in storms and fog."

"My condolences to their families."

"Don't concern yourself. That is my obligation."

"I agree," replied Lisianski, taken aback, but continuing. "As soon as we noted the separation, we doubled back. We hoisted signal lights and fired our guns. We spent the night and half the next day searching."

"Yes. Yes, of course. We, on the other hand, continued upon the course laid out. We assumed that the *Neva*, being the foremost of the two vessels, would remain on course at reduced speed, allowing us to overtake. In the event of detachment, in the future, I suggest you follow that course."

"Why did it take so long for you to reach the Marquises?" ventured Lisianski.

"If you recall, we had agreed that in the event of a separation, the *Nadezhda* would put in at Easter Island for at least a day."

"I deemed it prudent to proceed directly to Taiohae Bay and await your arrival here," replied Lisianski.

"We, assuming that the *Neva* was in the lead, remained at Easter Island some five days," Lisianski explained.

"All's well that ends well, but in future we should not allow such a distance to develop between the ships," concluded Kruzenstern.

"Certainly," said Lisianski, wondering if the pun was intended.

The verbal joust was over. Neither man was completely satisfied. Lisianski was too fine an officer to be insubordinate, but he would not allow an unwarranted attack on his judgment by an old classmate who had violated his own sailing plan.

Upon his return to the *Neva*, Lisianski found the king of the bay aboard with presents of fruit. There were many islanders swimming about the ship, including a number of women. Lisianski ordered the crew not to allow the women aboard until the ship was ready to sail. That evening at least one hundred women surrounded the ship. They let it be known with unself-consciously lewd gestures that they wanted to come aboard.

"Lieutenant Arbuzov," Lisianski directed, "don't allow these wantons on board."

"Captain, the men have not even seen a woman since St. Catherine's."

"Well, they are certainly seeing all of these. One should follow the exemplary behavior of Captain Cook and avoid the possible spread of disease."

"Sir, are we protecting the health of these innocents?" Arbuzov asked, gesturing ironically in the direction of the pleading, undulating ladies swimming absolutely naked around the ship.

"Some of them look extremely young."

"None of them look extremely innocent, sir."

This conversation was taking place over general pandemonium, lustful exchanges, and gestures between the crew and the ladies of the sea.

"All right, Arbuzov. I can't bear to look at those doleful eyes. The women may come aboard on two conditions: you must employ some ruse to persuade Father Gideon to go ashore for the night, and the women must be off the ship by dawn."

The alacrity with which the men arranged an ecumenical council between Father Gideon and the local witch doctor was astonishing. No sooner was the jolly boat out of sight than, as if by some silent signal, the boarding party took the ship by storm. The bacchanal continued through the night. There was, as Lisianski later wrote, "great gaiety, laughter, and good-natured wantonness." Just before dawn, the sea-maids tore themselves out of the arms of their lovers and splashed over the side, like schools of fish.

These sea nymphs shamelessly enjoyed sexual expression without the least stigma. Of course, the gallant men of the *Neva* answered the call to duty. Hand mirrors were the most popular token of their appreciation. The men wondered about the captain's activities but were too preoccupied to satisfy their curiosity. Each presented his darling with some small memento of the occasion; some became manifest months later.

Coconuts, breadfruit, bananas, and articles of curiosity were exchanged for pieces of iron hoop, axes, and knives. The king refused to take anything until he presented a canoe full of coconuts and a large pig. These were exchanged for a striped cap, an ax, three knives, a cock, and a hen. The king was fascinated by a large dressing mirror in the cabin; he spent a great deal of time in front of it making amusing and grotesque faces. At length he dove over the side and swam away, completely ignored by his subjects.

On the next day, the trading continued. The king came aboard. One of the sailors accidentally struck him on the head with an oar, and the king immediately fell down and made a wry face, as if in great pain. The seaman was reprimanded and, in compensation, he gave the king a small piece of iron. Immediately, the king began to laugh and let it be known that he had not been hurt at all. He appeared to enjoy the deception immensely and went ashore in high spirits.

Lisianski, Kruzenstern, and some thirty men went ashore to pay a call on the king. They made their way along a beach, where Lisianski noted pockmarks of shells in some of the palms, reminding him of the fate of kind and gallant Captain Cook on this island. They passed through groves of coconut and breadfruit trees. As they walked along the path winding about many springs of water, they accumulated a large crowd of curious natives.

The path was extremely pleasant. There was a beautiful view of the ships anchored in the bay. The small bay was wonderfully placid, being surrounded on all sides, except for a very narrow entrance, by hills and mountains covered with lush vegetation. A high, fresh waterfall adorned the south side, falling sixty feet into the lagoon.

Having deployed the troops, Lisianski and his men entered a building with a foundation of stone. The sides were made of moveable poles to admit air and light. The roof was thatched with leaves of breadfruit. The interior was divided into two parts; the back portion, which appeared to be the sleeping chambers, was covered with mats spread upon clean, dry grass.

Along the walls were hung domestic implements of calabash, stone axes, pikes, clubs, and other instruments of war. A large drum made of a hollow tree trunk and covered with sharkskin sat in a corner.

The king, queen, and a young woman, their daughter-in-law, greeted the Russians with polite ceremony. The young woman bore the title "Goddess of the Bay." All three were dressed in yellow cloth made from the bark of a tree. Their bodies were smeared with oil of coconut and yellow dye. Lisianski exchanged more gifts with the natives but refused to trade gunpowder.

On the night before the Russians' departure, a number of rockets were fired into the sky. The natives reacted with fear and excitement; they believed the ship had the power to launch stars that upon disappearing returned to the ship to be sent up again.

Lisianski made copious notes about the flora and fauna of the islands and the social structure of the inhabitants. He was particularly appalled with the honors paid to the priests upon their demise:

"The most barbarous honors are paid here to priests on their decease. I was assured that, on the death of a priest, three men must be sacrificed; two of whom are hung up in the burying ground, while the third is cut to pieces, and eaten by visitors; all but the head, which is placed upon one of the idols. When the flesh of the first two is wasted away, the bones that remain are burnt. The custom of the country requires that the men destined for sacrifice should belong to some neighboring nation, and accordingly they are generally stolen."

Lisianski observed that the natives were a handsome and well-made people. He also recorded the locations and amenities of the harbors and bays. He even compiled a small dictionary of their language for use by subsequent Russian captains.

On the morning of the seventeenth of May, while getting under way, the *Nadezhda* ran aground.

CHAPTER NINE

The rescue

Yaskadut walks through a summer meadow. The sky darkens as clouds roll. The earth shakes. Rain falls, turning to sleet, then snow. Creatures scurry for shelter. Howls, hoots, and screeches pierce the dark. Yaskadut steps into the woods. Trees sway and groan, grabbing at him. Stars shimmer and disappear. The full moon, shining through the trees, is obliterated by squalling sheets of snow. Wolves howl and bears grumble. Yaskadut shelters under the bough of an ancient spruce. Snowdrifts bury him.

He awakens to the sweet tinkle of icicles. He begins to dig out of his snow den. The sky glows as the aurora borealis glimmers lilac hues. Icicles collect starlight into twinkling blue jewels. Snow sparkles sapphire diamonds.

A shadow blocks the stars as Xietl stoops in a roar to the meadow. Trees shudder as he flares to the ground. Tl'anaxe'eda'kwaa alights from his shoulders onto the meadow. Iridescent hair hangs loosely down her back. Her nude body is translucent green. Her emerald eyes glow.

The air warms to a sunny day. The meadow greens as she dances and twirls in lavender paintbrush and crimson fireweed. Snowmelt trickles and rivulets sing. Songs of birds and insects fill the air.

Tl'anaxe'eda'kwaa beckons and Yaskadut stumbles to her embrace. Upon their touch, they ascend, to the sound of an enchanted flute. Up they whirl in blue sky among fleecy clouds, beyond the sun, into violet heavens.

Tl'anaxe'eda'kwaa and Yaskadut dance to the music of the heavenly bodies. Orbiting, spinning, celestial arrays resonate with the song of the universe, the beauty of being. Tl'anaxe'eda'kwaa and Yaskadut ascend the Milky Way, peopled by transmigrating souls of hunters and warriors.

Yaskadut greets the father he never knew. He looks upon his face and learns of his life, his sorrows and happiness. At last, when there is nothing more to share, they part until that time when they will meet again. Tl'anaxe'eda'kwaa takes Yaskadut's hand and bursts into a thousand fireflies, whirling with dizzying speed about his head as he settles to the meadow. He falls into sweet oblivion, lulled by the soothing and somber rhythm of rain.

Tl'anaxe'eda'kwaa speaks:

"Behold! I am Yesterday, Today, and Tomorrow.

"I am the First and the Last.

"I am the timeless infinite Present.

"Attend! I come to teach thee what is, what was,

"And what shall be.

"Beware! He who kills the bird, kills the song,

"And with the song—himself.

"Know! Not cold, not hunger, not pain,

"Not bristling teeth of danger,

"No mortal, nor even the jaws of death,

"Shall subdue thee."

Aataagliga kicked at the lumps of rumpled furs.

"What's this? Looks like dead Chugach. Many dead all piled up like a wall but all naked! Dumb Chugach! What happened to that great bird? Something strange here. I'll take the furs. Not needed now." Aataagliga, whose name meant "fur seal bull," mumbled to himself as he dug through the pile of fur clothing and snow.

"Aiiyyee! It moves!" He jumped back, dropping the sleeve that he had been tugging. "Somethin' alive here?"

He crouched and drew his big round head down between his hunched shoulders as he stepped forward to get a better look. He kicked the heap again. A low moan came from the pile of fur and ice.

"Who's that?" Aataagliga grew bolder and more curious. He pulled away the layers of frozen clothing, revealing Yaskadut's stiff blue body.

"Huh! That not Chugach. What are you? Where you from? What you doin' with these dumb Chugach?" Aataagliga asked as he uncovered Yaskadut. He immediately pulled out pieces of flint and iron. He poured dry sea grass from a mukluk onto a ragged parka, pooled seal oil on it, and struck a spark. Soon he had a fire going.

He pulled Yaskadut's mittens and boots off and erected a lean-to over him and the fire. He heated seal oil in a stone cup as he rubbed snow on Yaskadut's feet, hands, and face. When the oil was just barely warm, Aataagliga rubbed it all over Yaskadut's body.

"You dead? Say something! You not Anooshi, are you? Hate Anooshi but like chai. No. You not Anooshi but pretty ugly like them. Skin like sunset but long dogface. You want hot chai? I got some. Heat snow and pretty soon have chai."

Yaskadut moaned and moved, but he was a long time rousing. After a while, he sat up. His eyes widened as he saw the short fur-covered, bandy-legged man standing over him.

The man's head was too large for his body, with its short arms and legs. He had a big smiling face, with upper eyelids folded over the canthus in the inner corner of the eye, giving them an oblique appearance. His skin was windburned and ruddy. He sported snow-white mustaches that looked like walrus tusks. His shoulders and arms were powerful.

He wore a transparent gut outer garment that reached below his knees. A jaunty long-brim bentwood cap, decorated with sea lion whiskers and dentalia, sat on his head. Rows of beaded strings hung from the margins of his ears, and labret pegs adorned the corners of his mouth and lower lip, complemented by a dentalium shell through the cartilage of his nose. The old man was a picture of barbarous splendor. He grinned and said something in a language Yaskadut had never heard.

Yaskadut tried to speak, but his voice only croaked as his stiff face and cracked lips tried to move. The old man handed him a stone bowl full of some warm liquid. Yaskadut took it. Sniffed it and tasted it. The strong brown liquid warmed his throat all the way to his belly. He vomited.

"You a cannibal? I see you eat Chugach. Aaaggh!" Aataagliga made a face and spit in disgust. "I'd rather die. Those Chugach filthy."

"Who are you? Where am I?" asked Yaskadut.

The old man simply looked at him and shrugged. He waddled toward his qayaq. Yaskadut had never seen such a craft. It was snow white and translucent. He could see the frame and ribs through the skin. Its lines were as clean and neat as those of an Arctic tern.

Aataagliga reached inside and pulled out a freshly killed seal pup. He dragged it over the ice to the fire and began skinning it.

"Must eat. A little. Slow. Seal much better than Chugach."

He roasted small pieces of meat, stuck on a bone knife over the fire. He held out bite-size pieces to Yaskadut, who gratefully accepted. After three pieces, he threw up again.

"Keep trying. Soon keep some. You almost dead. Skin on toes white. Maybe turn black and fall off. When you get strong, we go home."

Yaskadut could not understand a word Aataagliga said, but his gestures were clear. He pointed to himself and said, "Yaskadut."

The old man smiled, and pointing to himself said, "Aleut."

Yaskadut had heard of people called Aleut who lived far out on the sea ice.

"No, no. I am not a Yaskadut. That is my name. I am Shee Atiká Kiks.adi of the Tlingit."

Upon hearing the word *Tlingit*, the old man jumped away from him and ran to the qayaq, where he grabbed a harpoon. He swung it toward Yaskadut and assumed a combative stance. Aataagliga knew that Aleut and Tlingit lived in a perpetual state of war.

"You Dog Man. You kill people on sight."

After eons of war, killing one another was a spontaneous reflex, not a reasoned position but a genetically learned response originating in a thousand years of conflict. They killed one another, instantly and without thinking. When an Aleut and a Tlingit met, an immediate and desperate struggle for life wordlessly and instantly commenced. Aataagliga took a step toward Yaskadut.

A shriek cut through the silence. Aataagliga dropped his harpoon and fell to the ice as a huge shadow passed overhead. Circling high above was the largest, most terrifying creature he had ever seen. Xietl transfixed him with blood-gorged eyes. Aataagliga went blind and fell unconscious.

Slowly, he recovered his senses and started, instinctively throwing his arms in front of his face. He peeked through his arms, searching for the terrifying image. He lay very still, afraid to move. Finally, he summoned the courage to speak:

"Tlingit are devils! Kill everything. Kill all the time. I leave now. I have no chai with Tlingit witch!" With those words, the old man crawled to his qayaq, shoved off with the double-bladed paddle, and disappeared among the waves.

Yaskadut groaned and fell back on his fur pallet. He passed out.

Thump! Thump! Aataagliga kicked the inert pile of furs.

"Hey, Tlingit! You give me furs, I'll take you to my village."

It had taken all of his courage and greed to return. He gave up the idea of killing the Tlingit. In fact, he was even afraid to have such a thought. The creature that looked like a great bird might know his thoughts.

Yaskadut roused himself. This time he tried speaking Chugach.

"You came back. I need help."

Aataagliga blinked and bobbed his head, continually swiveling to search the sky and shifting from one foot to the other.

"You speak like Chugach. First you eat Chugach, then you Chugach?"

"No. I'm not Chugach, I'm Tlingit."

Aataagliga flinched at the word.

"You Tlingit but eat Chugach. Now you have Chugach speech. Chugach talk like real people but names of things crazy."

Yaskadut despaired of explaining but was relieved to find a language that the little man understood.

"Will you take me off this ice floe to shore?"

"No. Not take you to shore. Take you to village, but you give me furs."

Yaskadut, although dulled by his ordeal, realized that the old man wanted to bargain. He gathered the clothing and personal effects of the dead. Aataagliga started another fire and brewed tea. Yaskadut and Aataagliga drank tea while Yaskadut bargained for his life. Aataagliga pointed to an object and Yaskadut begrudgingly handed it over. Aataagliga pointed to another and Yaskadut refused. Aataagliga started preparing to leave. At the last minute, Yaskadut conceded, and the process began anew. Eventually, Aataagliga had all the clothes, knives, and personal effects of the others. He pointed to Yaskadut's clothes.

Although, there are few swear words in Chugach, Yaskadut expressed his opinion of Aataagliga: "You are dog feces! You stink worse than whale's breath. You don't know how to hunt. You're only fit for bailing."

The latter comment struck home. Aataagliga threw all the clothes and personal goods he had obtained into the qayaq, seated himself, and pushed off into the icy sea. He paddled around and around the ever-diminishing ice floe, yelling in Inuit and waving his paddle angrily at Yaskadut.

"Don't have to trade. Just wait. You be dead soon."

On Aataagliga's third pass, Yaskadut yelled, "It is not true that you do not know how to hunt. You killed a seal and gave me some to eat."

Aataagliga paddled on around the ice floe, but returned. On this pass, Yaskadut said, "You handle that qayaq well. I am sure that you are a hunter, not a bailer. You are a real sea animal."

Aataagliga executed a sharp turn and drove his qayaq upon the ice. He gestured to Yaskadut to join him as he muttered, "I will take this Chugach-eating cannibal-Tlingit-dog-man to the village. Maybe he can be of some use."

Yaskadut gathered up his personal effects and dragged them behind as he staggered toward the qayaq. Aataagliga stepped on the ice and stuffed them into the qayaq, forward of the hatch. He motioned Yaskadut to enter through the hatch and lie aft, facing forward. Aataagliga stepped into the qayaq and grunted as he launched the heavily burdened vessel into the sea. Yaskadut could see the waterline through the hull. The qayaq wallowed almost up to its gunwales as the old man paddled toward the setting sun. The frame of the qayaq was made of whalebones, driftwood, and baleen neatly bound together with gut. The white, translucent skin was almost seamless. Even with the tremendous load, it flexed and moved with ease over the surface of the water.

The only concession Aataagliga had made to the presence of Russians in his village was to name his qayaq *Ptichka*, a Russian word meaning "little bird."

Sealskins covering the sole of the qayaq provided warmth. Out of the wind and snuggled in the furs, Yaskadut fell asleep. Aataagliga paddled and muttered to himself about witchcraft and great birds.

Aataagliga poked Yaskadut. "You know what Sila?"

Yaskadut groaned and replied, "No. What is Sila?"

"Sila is everywhere—a great power. Sometime it takes human or animal form and is called Tlam-Shua. Tlam-Shua is so powerful he does not speak in words. He speaks through gales, snowstorms, rain showers, and stormy seas. He will talk to children so gently they will not be scared. Then the child knows that danger threatens. The child tells his parents, and the shaman does what he can."

After a pause Aataagliga cunningly added, "I think that giant raven that screamed at me is Tlam-Shua. Tell him I won't hurt you."

Yaskadut knew nothing of a giant raven, but a vision of Xietl flashed in his mind. "Don't worry," he said. "He will do nothing as long as you behave."

Aataagliga grunted and kept on paddling and muttering. All night and into the next day he muttered, grunted, and paddled. At dawn Yaskadut awoke and asked, "How much farther? I can't breathe. I can't stand it in here."

Aataagliga replied, "Want out?"

Yaskadut fell silent and Aataagliga slipped a piece of smoked salmon under the hatch to him. "Only half day more."

They drifted as they ate. Aataagliga paddled toward the sunset along the Aleutian Island Chain. He avoided passing Korovinskaya Harbor on Atka by circling far out to sea to approach the backside of the island from the northeast.

He passed from the North Pacific to the Bering Sea between Atka and Great Sitkin Islands, then dawdled, waiting for low tide before closing with the island just at dusk. As the sun went down behind the island, he pulled hard directly for a sheer cliff. Within a few feet of the cliff, he paddled behind a rock face and into a hidden cleft between the rock and the cliff. At the base of the cliff, he pushed aside hanging seaweed and moss, exposing the small opening of a cave. He leaned back and pushed the qayaq through an entry that was only accessible at low tide. Years before, he had discovered the cave while pursuing a wounded sea otter.

The opening barely admitted the qayaq with Aataagliga pushing along the sides in a near-prone position. The cave was cramped and dark for twenty yards before it opened into a grotto with ledges covered in seaweed. The interior was dimly lit by rays of the setting sun, which glinted through a small moss-screened opening at the top of a domed interior.

A long, graceful fan of sun rays, tinted green from the moss, picked up the silver mist of a lace waterfall, producing a small rainbow. The surge of the sea and the singing waterfall soothed Aataagliga. He exhaled with relief.

The Tlingit will not reveal this place. Sila protects him. Raven is his friend. He will not like the Anooshi. He will not betray this place, he thought.

Although Yaskadut was still barely able to stand, he helped Aataagliga stow his beloved qayaq on a recessed ledge high above the waterline. First, the qayaq was washed in fresh water from the waterfall and wiped dry, and then the few seams that existed were thoroughly rubbed in seal oil that had been warmed over the stone lamp that was lit when the sunlight failed. After the paddle, harpoon, lance, throwing board, and darts were wiped down, they were wrapped in sealskins and placed inside the qayaq.

The two mortal enemies, Aleut and Tlingit, waited for darkness. Quietly, Aataagliga began to tell Yaskadut about his people:

"I tell you a little what I know, how people lived and how it is. This place is Atka. We had few wars. Our weapons were for hunting. We almost never killed people. We didn't steal. We didn't divide things up. If a man was usin' a thing, he used it; if he did not, another could.

"Before the Anooshi came, we had little disease. Now we have much. Some get sores from sleepin' together. There's more sickness in the chest. Burning red spots come on the skin. People die.

"The Anooshi made a big house they call a church. People get baptized there. We had lots a' food most a' the time, but now all the food, baidarki, qayaqs, lances, knives, boots, hides, gut parkas, everything kept in one big house where no one lives, just those things.

"When the Anooshi want us to hunt, they give out those things. They give out food too, but it is some stuff they call flour and biscuits. At first, the people would not eat that stuff, but soon they started to eat so they would not die. But it just a slower death. This is not good food and we don't get much.

"Long ago, the people had lots a' furs, but now there are not enough. The hides are all kept in the big house where no one lives.

"The Anooshi taught the people to put potatoes in the ground. That's their favorite food. They rot it and make vodka. The winters are long and hard now, not like the old days when we saved up food and sat in our long houses, eating, singing, dancing, and making babies until the weather got better.

"When spring comes, the Anooshi make all the men and boys hunt for the sea otter. Sometimes, they don't wait for spring. The men stay away for a long time, sometimes all summer. The women gather eggs and kill birds and fish, but when the men do not come back during the winter, the women and children starve." Aataagliga fell silent. He sat for a while lost in thought, then returned to his story.

"Whole villages of women and children on other islands died when the men were taken away and winter came. The strong men had to hunt even in the winter. The Anooshi always want the sea otter, more than anythin'.

"Sometimes they bring back a whole ship full. We fear there will be no more." Again, there was silence, but Aataagliga was not finished.

"If the men are gone all winter, the people die. Lots a' men don't come back from hunts, but when they come back, the Company puts out a big barrel of vodka. This is free for the hunters. They just hang cups on that barrel and stand around drinking and eating. The Company does this free.

"When the men come back, there is a whole big ship full of animal meat, hides, sinews. The intestines and all the stomachs are stored, dried, and filled with dried fish. The ocean fish and the river fish are stored in the big house, separate. Sometimes they give this out to the people, but never enough."

Yaskadut interrupted, "You have become slaves! Did you fight?"

"At first we thought they were humans and we saw their iron and muskets," Aataagliga said. "We wanted those things, so we traded for them, but they would not trade for muskets. We shared our wives with them.

"Soon they had all the furs they wanted. They wouldn't give nothin' for the new ones. We had no weapons for war, jus' for huntin', and they had muskets an' cannon. We thought those were magic. They kept our women and children separated from us and told us to hunt or there would be no food for them."

He paused again for a moment, then looked at Yaskadut.

"You will see."

CHAPTER TEN

Hawaii and Kodiak

The *Nadezhda* was not hard aground. At high tide she floated off. The ships sailed the great expanse of the North Pacific. Each day the Marquises fell farther astern. North by northeast they sailed, bound for the Sandwich Islands. The sights and sounds of land faded. Salt water and wind whitened the *Neva's* deck. All trace of land washed away as she rose and fell on the broad back of the greatest ocean in the world. The sun and sea burnished the men. The trivialities of shore life paled. The minds of the men drained of all but the most basic concerns: navigation, sail trim, ship's repairs, food, and sleep. The ship sailed smoothly as the crew functioned well in blissful preoccupation with the simple but profound demands of sailing and survival.

Sails were trimmed to obtain the maximum speed-on-course provided by wind direction, current, and surface waves. Day and night, they sailed to the sounds of the wind in the rigging, creaking lines, and slating canvas. The eternal sea rolled with a sigh. A great number of birds and fish surrounded the ship. On the eighth of June porpoises and frigate birds greeted her approach to the Sandwich Islands.

Lisianski ordered the anchors unlashed, eased over the side to the cat-heads, and shackled on the chains, ready for release upon drifting to a suitable anchorage. After setting the anchor, Lisianski repaired on board the *Nadezhda* to confer with Kruzenstern, who was waiting at the waist by the boarding ladder.

"Good afternoon, Ivan Fedorovich," Lisianski hailed him. "Permission to come aboard?"

"By all means, Captain-Lieutenant Lisianski," replied Kruzenstern.

Yurii was tired but elated with the successful landfall. It had been a long voyage across the vast and empty expanse between the Marquises and the Sandwich Islands. He was surprised by the formal address he received, but he stepped aboard, faced the stern and saluted the ensign, then turned sharply and saluted Ivan Fedorovich Kruzenstern, the captain of the convoy.

"Shall we confer in my cabin, Captain-Lieutenant Lisianski?"

"With pleasure, sir." Yurii sensed that the atmosphere aboard ship was tedious and formal. They left the waist and proceeded down the aft ladder to the captain's cabin. Yurii was surprised to see the expedition commander, Nikolai Petrovich Rezanov, in formal attire, awaiting his entry.

"Good afternoon, Commander Nikolai Petrovich. It is good to see you," greeted Lisianski.

Kruzenstern spoke first and without preamble.

"Captain-Lieutenant Lisianski, I am aware that the voyage was long and wearisome. I suggest that you and your men remain here for a short while to rest and recuperate. The *Nadezhda* will convey Count Nikolai Petrovich Rezanov to Japan. As you know, he is to serve as the first Russian ambassador to Japan. We will sojourn there in accord with our sailing plan and then sail on to Petropavlovsk, Kamchatsky. You recall we are to meet there before the return voyage to St. Petersburg."

"Thank you, sir, but my crew is in good shape, the ship is sailing well, and we would prefer to press on to Kodiak."

Kruzenstern grimaced at Rezanov but acquiesced. "As you wish, but you will need to resupply before you strike out on the last leg of this journey."

Yurii took his leave. He mulled over the situation in the longboat while returning to his ship. He was glad that he had declined the suggestion that he serve as the commander of the voyage; it was onerous to be told what to do in the most obvious circumstances. He congratulated himself on his good sense in deferring to his classmate Ivan Fedorovich. He would have been unhappy with the pompous diplomat Count Rezanov and the strained and formal atmosphere on board the *Nadezhda*.

Lisianski and his crew took ample time to resupply in the islands before striking for Kodiak. The *Neva* and *Nadezhda* parted ways near the big island of Hawaii at latitude 18° 58' and longitude 156° 20' on June 9, 1804. Appropriate regret was exchanged, but the word свобода ("freedom") came softly across the water. Yurii realized that the *Neva* was free to sail at her maximum speed. She could steer her own course; she could navigate without consultation and compromise. Deference to an expedition commander or convoy captain was no longer necessary. It was heady wine, especially intoxicating to the youthful Lisianski, who had always sailed under immediate naval command.

The *Neva* sailed alone upon the empty sea, an infinitesimal dot of humanity in a great desert of water. She carried the honor of the Russian Imperial flag.

On the eleventh of June, the *Neva* dropped anchor in the Bay of Caracacoa. Just before dark one hundred mermaids appeared. They swam around the ship exhibiting their glorious emblems of pleasure.

"Captain, may the women come aboard?" asked Lieutenant Arbuzov.

"Lieutenant, you exhibit profound lechery for one so young."

"Just an exuberance of life and duty, sir."

"Duty? Do your duties include servicing all the women of the Pacific?"

"Well, sir, I'm sure that no civilized European has ever denied these ladies the courtesy of a visit on board."

"Captain Cook did his best, and for good reason. He was concerned, not only for the health of the crew but also for the natives. He did not want to introduce venereal disease among these children of nature."

"But Captain, we are not the first ship to visit these islands."

"Nevertheless, we have not reprovisioned and there is much work to do. I will not give the ship over to debauchery."

"Perhaps we can entertain the ladies before our departure?"

"Perhaps, but for the present we shall have to risk affronting them. Let our guests know that we are not receiving just now."

"Aye, aye, sir."

The next morning canoes carrying a great variety of objects for trade surrounded the ship. Pigs, fowl, coconuts, sweet potatoes, taro root, and sugarcane were purchased with knives, axes, adzes, small mirrors, printed linen, coarse linen, scraps of iron, and barrel hoops. A boisterous commerce occupied the entire day.

Just before sunset, the now-familiar armada of nymphs besieged the ship. During the day, Yurii had seen evidence of venereal disease among the natives. He stood firm in his resolution. The siege was so desperate that he was forced to appeal to the local chief, who obligingly gave orders that all his people, male and female, were to disembark by sunset. The crew spent that evening quietly, if disconsolately, stowing supplies and mumbling.

On the following day, the thirteenth of June, trade continued at a brisk pace, but the natives no longer traded pigs or hogs for scraps of metal or barrel hoops. They demanded, at the least, good bars of iron.

Yurii entertained the chief, providing him with an ax, an adz, and three bottles of rum, in exchange for two pigs. The chief graciously invited Lisianski and his men to come ashore to feast with him. Yurii accepted the invitation.

The next day, several armed men accompanied Yurii ashore in a longboat. While passing along the shore, Yurii saw the scars of canister shot on the trees where Captain Cook's ships had vented their rage after his murder on the beach. Yurii felt the loss of a great navigator and a humane captain who had perished attempting to prevent bloodshed.

Lisianski noted the appearance of the people, their dwellings, and their furnishings. He inquired of their customs, history, religion, and daily habits. He even developed a rudimentary Hawaiian-Russian dictionary. He recorded the amenities of the islands, their geography, flora, and fauna. He closed his log entry with the following comments:

"I cannot take a final leave of these islands, without acknowledging that the inhabitants behaved in the most friendly manner to us, during the whole of our intercourse with them. Surrounded by hundreds every day, we never experienced the smallest injustice or injury; on the contrary, we had many proofs of their honesty and hospitality, which shows at least how much they have improved since the time of Captain Cook."

Upon his return to the *Neva*, Captain Lisianski was pleased to find three sailors from a North American ship on board. He had visited that country and got on well with Americans. They made friends easily and spoke freely about what was important to them, unlike the English, who were far more reserved. One of those sailors had spent time in the Pacific Northwest. He informed the captain that the natives had destroyed the Russian settlement in Shee Atiká.

"Surely not? Archangelsk? Do you know the details?" asked Lisianski.

"The Kiks.adi attacked on a Sunday afternoon. They donned fierce animal masks and were horribly painted. They fell upon the fort. Women and children screamed as fire forced the Russians to jump from the blockhouses upon waiting spears."

"But how did they overcome the defenses?"

"The Russians were all drunk and the native women had gained their confidence."

"Were there survivors?"

"Most were tortured and decapitated. Their heads were impaled on spikes in celebration. Some women and children were taken as slaves. A few Aleut, hunters for the Russians, escaped in boats."

Lisianski found it difficult to believe that the entire settlement had been destroyed, but he noted the details and resolved to help the victims and punish the perpetrators given the opportunity.

By the sixteenth of June, the *Neva* was fully provisioned and under way. Above the Tropic of Cancer, the winds were almost constantly westward. For that reason, Lisianski ordered the ship to steer northwest by north to accommodate the wind and make progress toward Kodiak. At latitude $25°$ North, the temperature dropped markedly. Warm clothes were issued, and the men were allowed rations of brandy.

On July 10, 1804, at a sounding of fifty-five fathoms with white sand and mud bottom, the snow-covered mountains of Kodiak appeared, bearing north by east, eighteen miles. By 16:00 the *Neva* passed Three Saints Harbor. The next day Cape Chiniatky was doubled. Entry into the harbor of St. Paul was painstaking, as it was well protected by islands and reefs.

The fort delivered an eleven-gun salute that was promptly answered. The anchor was let go. Several Russians put out from shore in baidarki, and the deputy commander of the settlement came aboard. The Russians warmly greeted their countrymen. Toasts were given to the first Russian crew to sail from St. Petersburg, Russia, to Kodiak, Alaska. Delight and satisfaction were steeped in a religious fervor of patriotism, gratitude, and vodka that lasted long into the night.

The island was surprisingly lush, covered with timber, ferns, peat moss, and berry bushes. Enormous brown bears ranging up to ten feet and 1,500 pounds roamed freely, feasting on salmon and berries. After exploration of the landfall and enjoying the generous party, Lisianski retired to his cabin. The strain of the long journey drained from his body. Tension gave way to the pleasant exhaustion of a difficult job well done. He slept soundly.

Within a few weeks, the *Neva* was surprisingly joined by the *Nadezhda*. The Russian diplomats had mistakenly assumed that an old invitation to send an envoy to Japan was still outstanding. Ambassador Rezanov was rudely rebuffed upon arrival and briefly imprisoned. After the abortive diplomatic visit, the *Nadezhda* sailed to Kodiak to winter over.

While living on board in well-sheltered Kodiak harbor, Ambassador Rezanov wrote a letter to the tsar, describing the wonders already performed on the Island of Kodiak:

"I should like to mention here how fortuitous trade is when it resides in such capable hands, but I shall not dwell upon this. This freedom will belong to future generations. For my part, I cannot find anything in my soul except to reveal to Your Excellency that when with God's help I reached Kodiak, I placed there, in eternal memory, the gifts that you have so generously entrusted to me, as well as your splendid letter to me and this inadequate response concerning my strong convictions. Let future generations know your concern for this land and my pride in being successful, that they may understand the value of my devotion.

"Count Aleksandr Sergeevich Stroganov sent various portraits, drawings, and maps for the Academy of Arts for the colony. The Minister of Naval Forces, Pavel Vasilevich Chichagov, sent plans of various ships, and His Eminence Metropolitan Amvrossii sent books for church services. The wishes of noted benefactors are being carried out. Many of the small boys who are being educated here have used and are still using these materials. Some of them have developed an inclination for drawing, and two of them, without instruction but only using pictures, have shown marked success in drawing portraits that bear striking resemblance to the subject.

"In the museum there are many mathematical, physical, and other instruments of rich English work. In addition, all ships are supplied with sextants, octants, and binoculars; chronometers and semichronometers are kept here for coastal use, as well as a theodolite, a circular instrument that is the work of Trouton. There is also an astrolabe and a very precise Jurgensen pendulum; also telescopes, fine binoculars, a large microscope, and an electricity machine, natural and artificial magnets, barometers, thermometers, charts, maps, atlases, and the like. The instruments that are kept in the museum represent a capital of twelve thousand two hundred and fifty rubles, not including those that are used on voyages."

Captain Lisianski later wrote to His Majesty, revealing a different view:

"The settlement of Kodiak has assumed the appearance of a European village. There are about thirty dwellings, a church, warehouses, barracks, and workshops for mechanical trades. Ambassador Rezanov even established a school for the instruction of the children in religion, reading, writing, accounts, and mathematics. However, he forgot to provide for the proper feeding of the students. These are about seventy of the best and brightest young men of the islands. When at home they were employed in fishing and hunting. They helped to support their families. As a consequence of the classes taught during the summer, less food is taken and prepared for the winter. Where there had been, if not abundance, an adequate supply of food for the winter, now supplies were low in Kodiak. The schoolboys had little to eat the whole winter while they studied accounting, European geography, and French.

"The island is becoming depopulated as those young men who do not attend the school are sent away on hunts for otter. The remaining population is largely old men, women, and children. For example, in the village of Toujajak there were a thousand able-bodied men, now there are only about forty. There had been many baidarki and baidari, now there are only four two-hatch baidarki and one baidar.

"I had occasion to examine a village on the nearby island of Afognak. Only women and children populated the settlement. The men were sent off hunting with a party led by Director Baranov in March. They had been away since the preceding spring. Insufficient amounts of provisions were laid in for the winter. The inhabitants were half-starved. I took pity on them and distributed the stock of dried fish I had in my boats. It was indeed a heartrending scene to see these emaciated beings crawling out of their huts to thank me for the trifling relief I had afforded them.

"The capable and compassionate Captain Bandar, superintendent of the settlement for the Company, has been replaced with a Promishlinik by the name of Prikatshchik. The following is an example of his administration:

"It must be noted that tall trees were at a premium since there were none on the islands. The few that wash up by the sea are carefully saved for years. They are used sparingly for absolute necessities, such as main supports for earth huts, baidarki, spears, and some household utensils.

"Prikatshchik summoned all the Russians from the islands to build a timber house, in the Russian style, for his use. All the wood was used for this project as well as the time and talent of the workers. Everything else came to a standstill until this edifice was completed."

Lisianski heard of other disturbing incidents. He noted them in his diary:

"Schelikov said he found fifty thousand inhabitants in the islands of Kodiak, Appoknak, Sachlido, Shujek, Tuckido, and Sichtunok in 1783. Director of the Company Delarov estimated that there were only three thousand in 1790. Schelikov either exaggerated, or forty-seven thousand inhabitants have disappeared. One hopes that the former is the case.

"The loss of men will lead to the extinction of the inhabitants and loss of a great resource to the Company. For example, last November a hunting party of one hundred and forty baidarki and three hundred Kolosh was sent from Shee Atiká to Kodiak. No one has heard of them since. I assume they were killed by Tlingits or one of the frequent violent storms that occur in that season.

"On an earlier occasion the English sent seven hundred baidarki with fourteen hundred Kolosh to Chatham Straits and Cross Sound where they hunted otter. They were then sent to Kodiak in October along the coast of Prince William Sound and Cook's River as far north as fifty-seven degrees of latitude. They were to return to Kodiak. This means that they would have ranged over sixteen degrees of longitude and three degrees of latitude. Bear in mind, there are sixty English miles in each degree. The expedition was conducted at a time when winter was well advanced. Between storms and starving, only thirty baidarki returned. Thus, the young men and boys of the Aleutians disappear, leaving old men and women with children to starve. I protest these pernicious practices and criminal waste. I will inform the directors of the Company."

These were the notes of the same man who later wrote of Kodiak residents:

"I found all the men sitting on the roofs of their houses. This is their favorite recreation after sleeping; though, they are also fond of sitting on the beach and looking for hours at the sea when they have nothing else to do. This practice resembles more a herd of beasts than an association of reasonable beings endowed with the gift of speech. Indeed these savages, when assembled together, appear to have no delight in the oral intercourse that generally distinguishes the human race, for they never converse; on the contrary, a stupid silence reigns amongst them. I had many opportunities of noticing individuals of every age and degree; and I am persuaded that the simplicity of their character exceeds that of any other people, and that a long time must elapse before it will undergo any very percep-tible change. It is true that on my entering their houses, some sort of ceremony was always observed by them; but by degrees even this so completely disappeared that an Aleutian would undress himself to a state of nudity, without at all regarding my presence; though at the same moment he considered me as the greatest personage on the island."

Lisianski had occasion to speak through an interpreter to a Chugach who had been captured by the Aleuts:

"Are your people peaceful?"

"Yes. We hunt. We don't make war."

"There are some Promishliniki among you, are there not?"

"Yes. At Pulagvik there is now a trading post, but the church was burned."

"How did that happen?"

"A few seasons ago a Russian priest came and built a church. He talked to the people. He told the people that they were bad and had to change their ways. He started telling them they had to go to church all the time. They had to get married in the church. They had to give up all but one wife. They had to be baptized or they would go to hell. He told them that their ancestors were heathens and were in hell and that the old ways were bad and evil. He got crazy. Some people believed him. Some did not. Some said they did not know which wife to give up. Some said they would not give up any. They started fighting among themselves. He made a big mess, so the people talked it over. They killed him and burned the church. It is quiet now. Russians can come and trade, but priests are not welcome. They will get killed. The people have decided there will always be war with Russian priests."

"How did you come to be here among the Aleut?"

"Some of our men went out hunting. They got lost, so we went to look for them. My uncle Aataagliga and his slave were among the lost ones. A big storm came and I separated from the others. These Aleuts caught me. I have been here ever since. They treat me like a dog."

CHAPTER ELEVEN

Aataagliga the Aleut

After Aataagliga revealed what had happened to his people, there was silence. He and Yaskadut sat in the gloom waiting for darkness. Yaskadut finally spoke: "Why are you going back?"

"That's home. My ol' woman's there an' the gran'kids. Most o' the men are gone. I stay and help. Many think they Anooshi. At Atka, Kanaga, Adak, Sitkin, Amalia, and Kodiak, they baptized many people. They made many Christians round there."

"What will you do when you get back?"

"Nothin'. I'll trade them these filthy Chugach clothes."

"What will you do with me?"

"Dun' know. Maybe trade ya for vodka."

Yaskadut was too weak to fight or run. Aataagliga giggled and suddenly asked, "Ya see that great bird? I saw him from far away. Could not believe my eyes so I followed him. He led me to you. Was he Yel the raven?"

"I did not see Yel," answered Yaskadut, but he thought of Xietl.

The two mortal enemies quietly talked into the night about a cataclysmic event: the arrival of beings from another world, against whom resistance seemed futile. They were terrifying, evil monsters that killed with iron, gunpowder, and disease while they infiltrated, insinuated, and consumed.

Aataagliga had seen iron before, when some flotsam from a Japanese ship had drifted ashore. In it, he found a long iron rod embedded in wood. He carried it home, lay down in his entryway, and let others step over him for good luck as he clutched the iron. A man with a piece of iron could make a blade that was sharp and held its edge, fashioning a lance that would never shatter or split on impact. It was the most precious of possessions. Striking it on flint could bring fire. It was stubborn and hard to make, but it held shape and could be sharpened by rubbing it against stone.

The Russians had an abundance of iron. They could shape it with fire into almost anything. It was better than bone, ivory, horn, wood, slate, or even copper. It was as hard as obsidian but not brittle. A hunter with a piece of iron was a better hunter. There was no match for it in battle. Iron was cold—indifferent.

Aataagliga did not blame iron, just as he did not fault the sea or the weather. Unlike the sea or the weather, however, iron could be taken in hand and used by men. Aataagliga treasured iron although it changed his life. Gunpowder was entirely beyond his ken.

When darkness had completely fallen, Aataagliga and Yaskadut slipped through the moss-covered opening at the top of the cliff. They stole through moonless gloom to the village on the other side of the island. It took all of Yaskadut's strength to stumble along behind Aataagliga.

The sod-roofed driftwood houses were set into the ground. The roofs were truncated pyramids resting on four central poles surrounding a smoke hole. The entry was through an anteroom and a sunken passage below the level of the main room; it was necessary to crawl through the passage. These features trapped heat in the main room. Inside, dirt platforms lined the walls. Separate rooms were used for sleeping and sweat baths.

Aataagliga led the way, with Yaskadut close behind. They crawled through the entry, skirted an open fire pit in the main room, pulled off their clothes, and crawled into Aataagliga's sleeping room. There was a grunt of reception, the sleeping furs were lifted, and the two joined Aataagliga's naked wife.

Aataagliga quickly began snoring. As Yaskadut lay wondering what the morning would bring, he felt a soft, warm body snuggle up to him. Smooth hands began to caress his loins. He was too exhausted, sleepy, and bewildered to move as Aataagliga's wife mounted and took her pleasure. The dreamy warm caresses soothed and delighted him. Anxiety left his body, and he too was soon asleep in the arms of his gentle but insistent suitor after his first experience of intercourse. The dull resonance of iron on pipe rousted the slumbering village. Aataagliga crawled over his wife and Yaskadut. He pulled on his clothes as he tugged on Yaskadut's big toe.

"Get up! Get up! It is the Company bell. We must assemble at the big house. Report for work detail."

Yaskadut opened his eyes and stared straight into the tattooed, round, toothless face of his lover, Kakuas-Geti. She was older than his mother. He blanched, rolling quickly away as her eyes flew open. She also recoiled in horror, screaming, as she threw her hands before her eyes to hide the vision of the strange, angular, un-tattooed, unadorned, naked face of the devil. She scrambled to the back of the room and pulled sleeping furs over her head, screaming, sobbing, and trembling. Slowly she calmed and lowered the furs, caught sight of Yaskadut, and screamed once more in horror, loud enough to bring the entire village on the run.

"Shut up! Shut up, ol' woman!"

"What is it? What is it?" demanded Kakuas-Geti.

"It's a Chugach cannibal I found on the ice."

"You ol' walrus cock! You fed me to a cannibal!" she shouted as she charged.

Aataagliga beat a hasty retreat through the entry tunnel but crawled directly into several villagers crawling to the rescue. A great babble rose from the tunnel.

Yaskadut, grabbing his parka and one mukluk, scampered up the notched log propped in the corner of the smoke hole and out onto the roof, then tumbled down into the stampeding village. The appearance of the thin, naked, dark-skinned creature, dragging his clothes, caused the crowd to shrink back, agape.

The report of a musket transfixed Yaskadut. He glanced toward a large building. A figure, trailing a cloud of smoke, was running toward him. This thundercloud bristled with metal buttons, a shiny long knife, and a musket. It shouted in a language he had never heard. Several more, just like it, tumbled out of the big house.

Sergeant Bezchestnik took command of the situation: «Кто идёт? стой! Остановись!» (Who goes there? Stop! Stop!)

The Russians herded Yaskadut to the big house, followed by the amazed villagers. Sergeant Bezchestnik spoke Aleut:

"Who are you?"

"I am Yaskadut, Kiks.adi Tlingit of Shee Atiká."

The word *Tlingit* caused a collective gasp among the Aleut.

"You are not Aleut. You are Tlingit?"

Even though Sergeant Bezchestnik could not pronounce the difficult word *Tlingit* correctly, Yaskadut understood the attempt.

"Yes. I am Tlingit."

The assembled Aleuts began to mutter, "Kill him! Kill him!"

Bezchestnik turned to the Aleuts.

"What tribe is the Tlingit? Where are they from?"

Aataagliga answered, "We know of Tlingit. They live that way behind the morning sun. We call them the 'Dog Men' because they are ugly and they kill everything. No talk. No trade. Just kill! As soon as they see a human, they kill him."

"Are there many of these Tlingit?" Bezchestnik asked no one in particular.

"No one knows. No one who goes there comes back. But we think they are as many as fish in the sea."

"How far away do they live?"

"We don't know. We don't go there."

Bezchestnik focused on Yaskadut. "Are there sea otter where you live?"

Yaskadut was stunned into awe by these creatures with their muskets and iron, but he suddenly heard the voice of Tl'anaxe'eda'kwaa: "Beware! Beware! Protect the people—all the people. The otter, the salmon, the Tlingit."

"I know nothing of otter that live in the sea."

"How did you get here?"

Aataagliga chimed in, "He sailed on ice. He made a sail of Chugach. He made a house of Chugach, and he ate Chugach."

In time, the Russians and Aleuts of Atka grew accustomed to their amicable cannibal. He was pressed into the work force just like all the other men of the island. The Russians treated the Tlingit no better or worse than the Aleut. They were all called "Kolosh."

Aataagliga was angry with Kakuas-Geti for making love to the Tlingit. The village women were, in turn, angry with him, because he gave vent to his rage after the fact. They said that he should have prevented it. Now it was done and he was only causing trouble for nothing. Kakuas-Geti was angry because she had assumed that the body in the dark was an Aleut guest, in which case nothing unusual had occurred. She was indignant and repulsed at the sight of Yaskadut's unadorned face and the thought of having shared her favors with a Tlingit, especially one who ate Chugach. But in time, both Aataagliga and Kakuas-Geti ceased bickering about the incident.

Not all of the Russians were cruel to the Kolosh. The Company policy was one of deference to local customs and religion while supporting attempts to save the souls of the heathen. The Company tolerated, even encouraged, intermarriage between the Promishliniki and the natives. Some Russians married Aleuts and begot children who drew the older Aleuts into the Russian sphere of influence. The Russians demanded that every male between the ages of sixteen and fifty work for the Company for at least three years. The Russian intelligentsia romanticized the "noble savage," while the Company destroyed his nobility.

Compared to the attitudes of the Spanish, English, and Americans, the Russians were enlightened, but their economic demands were relentless. The sea otter pelts were called "soft gold." They were composed of guard hairs and a rich, glossy undercoat of pellucid blue-black hair. The rare luster of the fur caught the light and glistened silkily. The pelts ranged in size from five to eleven feet. In addition to being considered one of the most beautiful, it was the most durable of all furs. In China, a trader could obtain the equivalent of one hundred dollars for each pelt. A year's hunt could produce two or three thousand pelts. The promise of such vast wealth drove good men to do bad things and bad men to atrocities.

Some Russians became skillful hunters and kayakers, but never at the level of the Aleuts. The Russians had a saying: "You could not tell if God invented the baidarka for the Aleut or the Aleut for the baidarka."

An Aleut in a baidarka became a separate, distinctive marine mammal, moving in the sea with the grace and beauty exhibited by the seal in its underwater ballet. Once Aataagliga told Yaskadut the following story:

"There was this one UluqidaX. He lived at SagiX. He had a cousin called SimludaX. Once they went into the sea for hunting. At Unimak Pass they halted. They killed many fur seals and loaded up the baidarki. On the way home a storm broke out and it got dark. The waves separated them. UluqidaX heard the baidarka of SimludaX speak to its master: 'Thou art in a danger and so be it. I shall not carry thee to safety, because when thou getest up in the morning from thy conjugal bed, thou dost not rub thy skin against me in order to share with me the warmth of thy wife's body.' Later UluqidaX heard his own baidarka speak: 'Don't trouble thyself, I shall carry thee to the shore because when thou getest up from thy wife thou sharest with me the warmth of her body.' Then those two were separated again by the waves. UluqidaX called and called but he heard nothing, so he went to SagiX. Next day, the weather was calm, so he searched for SimludaX. He saw something in the seaweed. He thought it was a log but it was SimludaX's broken baidarka. The hatch was split in two, and SimludaX was inside, dead. UluqidaX towed it to shore. He took SimludaX out and fixed the hatch. He put SimludaX back, tied him in with the waterproof skirt around his waist, and attached sealskin floats on both sides. He towed the baidarka back to SagiX, where he took his sister-in-law and her baby boy to see SimludaX. UluqidaX held the boy up by his pants so he could see SimludaX and said, 'When thou wilt marry, thou wilt have to communicate with thy baidarka by rubbing against her with the warmth of the body of thy wife after leaving her bed.' Then he returned the crying boy to his mother and said to his sister-in-law, 'Teach thy boy that when he will marry, not to have his wife for himself only and to include a partner in his marriage-union, his baidarka. Look at thy dead husband and do not expose thy son to the same fate.'"[3]

*   *   *

Before the Company, there had been no rank or class in the village. No government or state existed to restrict liberty. There was a community based upon the commonweal of a free people. There were so-called strong men who, others tacitly admitted, were superior hunters and thinkers. They were allowed to make suggestions, but cooperation was strictly voluntary. There was only one great rule: No one could avoid the struggle for food and clothing.

Trapping grounds and hunting fields were the property of all and none. Not even as a group did the Aleut lay exclusive claim to these places. The spoils of the chase did not exclusively belong to anyone, but were shared. Things used for the benefit of several families, such as communal houses and stone weirs for salmon fishing, belonged to the society. Personal possession depended upon actual use. A man not using a fox trap must allow another to use it. Some personal objects such as clothing, baidarki, sledges, and hunting weapons were respected. Violations of the right of possession were, however, not matters of significant concern. Theft and robbery were practically unknown, excluding pilfering from strangers.

Justice was not executed out of a sense of propriety; the emphasis was upon peace within the community. Occasionally, a settlement would combine to kill a man or a woman suspected of evil witchcraft. Such a person was a menace to the peace of the society. They might combine to kill a wild and brutal man or even

---

3   That is the equivalent of $4,575 a pelt in 2010 U.S. dollars.

an old or sick person who was a burden on the group, but there was no element of punishment, merely a need to maintain the peace and security of the village. Another method of maintaining the group was to send a person away. Banished from the village, he would become known as the "Outside Man," shunned and feared by all, having lost his "place" in society.

Those disputes that did occur were frequently settled by assembling the people to witness adversaries singing lampoons in verse so disparaging that the object of ridicule would rue the day and mend his ways. The stultification of common disapproval had a profound effect in small, isolated communities.

Yaskadut learned of one event that taught him a great deal about the Aleut. A man had killed another to obtain his wife. She had a baby boy at the time. The killer lovingly raised the boy, knowing that some day that boy would be required to exact a blood vengeance. The village did nothing, for the killer was a good husband and father. There was peace. The killer grew old waiting, seemingly unconcerned, for the day of his death. It came swiftly when the boy reached manhood.

Yaskadut would never forget his first sea otter hunt with the Aleut. There was an abundance of sea otter in the waters of the Aleutians. The two-hatch baidarka was used, with the hunter sitting in the forward hole, the paddler behind. As many baidarki as possible would gather for the hunt. Hunters used lightweight spears 125 centimeters long with barbed heads made of bone. A thick braid of sinew attached the head to the shaft one-third of the length from the three-feathered end. A throwing board, called an atlatl, was used to propel the spear with tremendous force.

Aataagliga, with Yaskadut in back, set out. They were accompanied by eight other baidarki. They paddled along the coast of an island, watching for sea otter. Aataagliga sang his hunting song:

"Why am I no longer able?

"Why cannot I now make a kill?

"What prevents me? What prevents me?

"Hither, my quarry!"

An otter was spotted. The closest baidarka launched a spear at the otter, but it twisted, rolled, and dove, and the shaft missed. The boat moved quickly to the spot where the otter had disappeared and a paddle was raised to signal the spot to the others. The other baidarki quickly formed a circle with the raised paddle in the middle. The radius of the circle was about the distance a healthy otter could swim before it must surface to breathe.

The otter surfaced not far from a baidarka in the circle. It was a female with a pup. Another spear was thrown. The otter grasped the pup and rolled, shielding the pup. It struck her in the back and dislodged as she dove once again. The nearest baidarka paddled to the spot and raised his paddle. The others formed a new circle but not quite so large. They knew the pup could not stay down as long as an adult and that the mother would be forced to surface.

The process continued for about an hour. Finally, the exhausted otter surfaced within six feet of Aataagliga, who immediately struck the pup with his spear. The pup whimpered as Aataagliga pulled it into the baidarka and retrieved his barbed shaft. The mother would not dive. She swam straight for the baidarka, crying in great distress. She swam around and under the baidarka searching for her pup. Aataagliga struck with a lance, thrusting it through her throat just below the chin. So intent on the pup was she that she did not even attempt to evade the thrust.

Aataagliga grunted as he pulled her aboard, "You get the pup first, mama will not leave. If she has two, she gives one to save the other. If the pup is big enough to escape, she will take the hit. If they dive, you watch bubbles. Underwater, they swim upstream or against the tide."

Distressed, Yaskadut said nothing.

Aataagliga added: "You let this pup and his ma live, your family may die."

Once Aataagliga killed a ringed seal. He took it home.

Kakuas-Geti no longer screamed at the sight of Yaskadut; rather, she greeted him with a toothless grin. She immediately poured fresh water on the seal's snout, explaining that he lived in salt water and therefore suffered from thirst. That night she placed the spear next to an oil lamp to keep "the soul of the seal warm."

Aataagliga commented, "Greatest danger in life is man eats souls. The soul of the prey must be respected." Yaskadut understood this sentiment. He felt the same about his animal brothers.

Life was good for both Aataagliga and Yaskadut. Aataagliga was finally considered too old to hunt otter for the Russians, and Yaskadut was not skillful enough, so they were left largely on their own. The waters around the Aleutians swarmed with rookeries of sea lion, fur seal, and otter.

In the summer when the salmon and trout came, the streams and creeks were dammed at low tide with stone weirs. The concentrated fish were taken with spears and leisters.

When the weather forced everyone indoors, the time was spent making and repairing gear, clothing, and utensils. Bone and ivory were carved with great skill into functional ornaments. The toggle of a mitten clasp might be a ptarmigan, the haft of a knife a trout. A seabird might be the buckle for a nape-thong of a baidarka frock. These objects not only delighted the eye of the beholder but also pleased the animals. The animals were less reluctant to die when killed with well-made weapons. Such weapons had magical qualities.

Eventually, Yaskadut became a good hunter, widely respected by the Aleut community. On one occasion, Kua, a young man, approached Yaskadut with a blue fox pelt.

"I know you are a Tlingit and an eater of Chugach," he said, "but you are healthy and a good hunter. I have not seen you eat anyone. You know our language and the way we live. My young wife is barren but I wish to have a son. Even though you are extremely ugly, my wife has consented. Will you make 'Ayi with child? There is no shame. She is a married woman." Yaskadut recognized the request for the great honor it was and accepted the blue fox.

As night fell Kua's wife, 'Ayi, kneeled down and crawled through the entrance of Aataagliga's house. She crawled on her hands and knees into the sleeping room. Kakuas-Geti was waiting in the dark room and welcomed 'Ayi onto the sleeping furs. Kakuas-Geti was there to introduce 'Ayi to Yaskadut.

Both women lay nude on the furs as Kakuas-Geti began to caress 'Ayi while speaking to her soothingly. Yaskadut entered after 'Ayi was relaxed. He disrobed and lay between the women, as instructed by Kakuas-Geti. There in the darkness, Kakuas-Geti, with her hands and mouth, aroused the two young lovers and assisted their intercourse, joining in on occassion. She enjoyed the role and looked forward to the baby that they would have. The night passed in murmurings and sighs in the darkness as Yaskadut was roused to the occasion in a variety of ways, while unable to discern the provider of the pleasure of the moment.

CHAPTER TWELVE

The "Koloshi"

Lisianski described the baidarka: "The Aleut men deserve great credit for invention of the baidarka, which is lightly constructed of wood, fastened together with whalebone, and covered over with sealskins, the seams of which are so well sewn that not a drop of water can get through. The baidarki paddle very fast, and are safer at sea in bad weather than European boats, especially when provided with good hatchway cloths, which are always drawn over holes, answering to hatchways, and extended round the waists of the people sitting in them.

"It is common to send one of the crafts from Kodiak to as far as the Island of Oonalashka, or to Sitca Sound. For such voyages, however, the rowers must be furnished with new camleykas, which they always fasten tight round the neck and arms, as a guard against the waves of the sea, which often roll over them. When there are several of these vessels in company, and a storm overtakes them, they fasten together in parties of three and four, and thus ride it out, like so many ducks tossed up and down by the waves, without the smallest danger. At first, I disliked these leathern canoes, on account of the bending elasticity in the water, arising from their being slenderly built; but when accustomed to them, I thought it rather pleasant than otherwise—"

"Ahoy, the ship! Permission to board?"

"Granted."

"Captain Lisianski. I have an urgent matter to discuss with you," said the deputy commander of the settlement, handing Lisianski a document describing the destruction of Archangel by the Kiks.adi of Shee Atiká in the previous year.

"I beg you, Captain, go to the rescue of those poor devils that remain and avenge the deaths of sixty Christian souls. We have anxiously waited for help. Mr. Baranov left for Shee Atiká this spring with four small ships, one hundred and twenty Russians, three hundred baidarki, and eight hundred Kolosh. He is still there and may need assistance."

"I will depart as soon as possible."

"Thank you, sir. I'm sure that Alexander Alexandrovich will be grateful."

The *Neva* was unloaded in pouring rain. Easterly winds pinned the ship in the harbor until the fifteenth of August. On that day at 17:00 the wind shifted and she departed for Shee Atiká. A strong offshore breeze blew the fully dressed ship on a broad reach down the coast to Mount Edgecumbe. A cone-shaped snowcapped peak came into view, sitting on a cape marking the northwest entrance to Shee Atiká Sound at latitude 57° 02' North and longitude 135° 08' West. The *Neva* entered the sound with the tide and anchored in fifty-five fathoms, with a clay bottom, at 22:00 hours.

"Novo Arkhangelsk Krepost is located at 57° ' latitude. The mouth of Sitca Sound is not less than twenty-five versts (16.5 miles) wide and extends inland by almost the same distance. The shoreline is dotted with numerous wooded islands, many providing excellent harbors with good bottom and sufficient depth to make safe anchorage. It is possible to enter and leave from any direction, providing ready entry and egress before almost any wind. From our entrance into Sitca Sound, the place where we now were, there was not to be seen on the shore the least vestige of habitation. Nothing presented itself to our view but impenetrable woods, reaching from the water-side to the very tops of the highest mountains. I never saw a country so wild and gloomy; it appeared more adapted for the residence of wild beasts, than men," Lisianski wrote.

A fog-shrouded morning greeted the ship. A small canoe with four natives drifted into view. Their approach was tentative; they stood off just at the edge of bow and arrow range.

"Small boat approaching to starb'rd, sir."

Lisianski walked to the rail and observed the natives with a glass.

"What do they want?"

"I don't know, sir. They have been there for about one half-hour."

Lisianski beckoned for the men to approach, but they hesitated. The fog began to burn off. A baidar appeared, making its way across the sound toward the ship. The natives quickly paddled their boat to the far shore.

The sun burned through the fog, revealing surrounding mountains. The shoreline was covered with heavy timber. The air was absolutely still. The sound was smooth-rolling molasses. The silent beauty was ominous. The baidar came alongside. The crew were Russians from the Company's vessels *Aleksander* and the *Ekaterina*. They had arrived some ten days earlier from Yakutat Bay and were awaiting Baranov's return from an otter expedition. There was nothing for the *Neva* do but wait as well.

The Russians informed Lisianski that the Kolosh had destroyed Baranov's fort on the hill overlooking the settlement and opposed the reestablishment of a Russian fort. No sooner had the Russians taken their leave than the strange canoe reappeared.

"Feodor Egorov, load the guns with grapeshot and kept at the ready. Let's see what these buggers are up to."

"Aye, grapeshot, sir."

The natives came within hailing distance and gestured that Captain Lisianski should come ashore to their settlement. When it became apparent that he would not, they held up two otter pelts and gestured toward a musket that they held aloft.

"They want to trade pelts for muskets. Well, we will have none of that. Look! Their faces are painted black and red. One has a black circle from his forehead to his mouth and his chin is red. They look like monsters." Lisianski was becoming alarmed at the mysterious and sullen behavior of the Kolosh. Frustrated by mutual fear, the natives eventually paddled away.

On the morning of the twenty-fifth of August, the *O'Cain*, an American ship, entered the sound, dropping anchor within sight of the *Neva*. On the afternoon of the following day, three Tlingit came alongside the American ship. A crewman from the *Aleksander* told the captain that one of the young men visiting the *O'Cain* was a relative of Yaskadut, the greatest enemy of the Russians among the Kolosh. After some discussion, Lisianski was persuaded to capture and interrogate this young man.

"Prepare the jolly boat, Lieutenant Arbuzov. As soon as they leave the *O'Cain*, overtake them. Take ten armed men. Use force if necessary," ordered Lisianski.

The young Tlingit saw the jolly boat closing on them. The race was on. Lisianski stood on deck and watched with his glass. At the nearest approach, shots were fired by the men aboard the jolly boat.

The Tlingit promptly returned fire as they increased speed and easily outdistanced the jolly boat in their three-hatch baidarka.

On the thirty-first of August, a large baidar with twelve naked men passed in the distance. The men's faces were painted and their hair powdered with feather down.

"Looks like they are after our fishing party."

"Gunner, fire a round in the direction of those Kolosh."

The shot fell harmlessly short as the baidar passed a small inlet and took shelter among the islands. That afternoon the captain of the *O'Cain* was attacked while returning from the woods. Lisianski promptly dispatched the armed launch under the command of Lieutenant Petr Povalishin.

"Give them a taste of the swivel guns, Lieutenant."

Seeing the approach of the launch, twenty Tlingit raced to their baidarki and cast off. The launch pursued, firing its bow gun. The Tlingit returned fire with muskets. Even with a fair breeze, the sloop-rigged launch could not overtake the baidarki; they paddled in excess of eight knots over shoals and into another bay beyond, where even the shallow-draft launch could not follow. Once over the rocks the Tlingit stopped and taunted the Russians, firing their flint-locks so effectively that several shots struck the launch. It withdrew and returned to the ship.

The commander of the *O'Cain*, Jonathan Winship, made for the *Neva* in his launch. It had been riddled. One ball had passed through the collar of the captain's greatcoat during the attack. He came on board in a rage.

"Thank you, sir, for your kind assistance. Those damned savages almost killed me. Where the hell did they get those flintlocks?"

"Very likely from some Boston trader, sir."

"Be that as it may, I'm leaving this place. My trading is finished. It is not possible to trade, what with this mess you Russians have stirred up."

In the morning, the *O'Cain* set sail. The days passed peacefully. Captain Lisianski had very little to do on board ship. Despite the hazard, he went ashore with an armed party to explore. He even fraternized with a few of the apparently friendly natives. He spent several days in close observation, duly noting the results in his diary. He described the land:

"Here one finds massive mountain cliffs, deep ravines, and wet tundra covered with a primal forest. There is an abundance of huge spruce trees. Many are up to one hundred and fifty feet high and six feet in diameter. They are straight and with few limbs in the lower trunk. This is excellent wood for shipbuilding, masts and spars. The natives make canoes of a single tree of red cedar up to fifty feet long, four and one-half feet in the beam and three feet in depth. Such canoes can hold thirty to forty people.

"The eroded granite cliffs support scarcely any soil but are covered with dense moss, and a lush growth of conifers. Old trees blown down by strong winds have rotted, giving rise to new growth; all together this comprises a dense impenetrable cover for wild animals. The principal forest tree of the conifers is the fir, then the larch, then a variety of cypress with a pungent odor. Small pines grow sparsely here and there. In the deciduous forests one finds alder, willow and the so-called apple tree. Low growing bushy vegetation with berries includes; the raspberry, which has a very watery flavor, the mountain ash, currant, blackberry, which also has an inferior flavor, elderberry, and many others. One plant belongs to the thorn family and is covered with countless razor-sharp thorns that are concealed below big harmless-appearing leaves. These plants

wreak havoc upon the unwary and discourage passage by the knowledgeable. It grows between forested areas along the shore and adds
to the impenetrability of the forest. It is know as the Devil's Club
for good reason.

"Along the shore, there is a shrub that produces good berries
called 'velvet berries.' In the tundra, grow cowberries, crowberries,
cranberries, and cloudberries. The root valerian is used like ginseng.
Medicinal herbs include melifolium. Wild grasses are gathered in
the spring and are used for food. These include young nettles, pars-
ley, sorrel, and chicory. The Kolosh also gather a fine moss that
grows on the rocks in the mountains. They use it to make a dye to
color the wool of the mountain ram, from which they weave blankets that only distinguished elders, or leaders called toyons, have the
right to wear."

On one occasion, Lisianski took a small party and climbed
Mt. Edgecumbe. He described the summit: "The views from this
summit were the most beautiful in nature. Innumerable islands and
straits, extending to the very entrance of Cross Sound, while the
continent stretching itself far and wide towards the north, lay under
our feet; the mountains, on the other side of Sitca Sound, appeared
as if reposing on clouds that hung motionless at their base. To add
to the enchantment, the sun, after a shower of a few minutes, shone
forth in all its luster."

On another day, he visited a mineral bath situated on the east
shoreline of Shee Atiká Sound, north of a group of small islands. A
hot spring of about 150 degrees flowed from the hillside into a large
basin that had been fashioned of wood and stone by the Tlingit. The
manganese- and salt-laden water was cooled to about 105 degrees
in the basin. It was possible to sit on the stones and look out over the
sound from the hillside at snow-capped peaks. A rudimentary shelter

was erected on the uphill side. Lisianski and his men sat in the warm water and listened to the sound of the rainfall on the wooden roof while they drank hot tea.

Several days passed as they waited for Baranov. Growing bolder, Lisianski led an expedition to the empty village of Shee Atiká. He later described the houses in great detail: "The houses of the Tlingit village are occupied only during the late fall and winter, after the hunting and fishing seasons. They were more than solidly built shelter against the cold. The location of the house symbolizes the inhabitant place in lineage. Each house is named. They are objects of beauty and pride. Many related families live within a house. The male owner is the House Chief. Any member of a household can claim hospitality and shelter in these large houses that contain up to sixty men, women, children, and slaves.

"The houses are rectangles over fifty feet long. The framework of the house is provided by four very large interior posts that support beams, two feet in diameter. The rafters are poles six inches in diameter. Above these poles are two layers of longitudinal planks running the length of the roof, parallel to the main beams. These planks are two-by-twelve inches. A few lines of parallel logs are laid over the roof planks. Holes are drilled through them, so they can be held in place with wooden pegs that are driven into the underlying rafters. The external walls are built of four-foot-wide, six-inch-thick planks, set vertically into the ground. The tops are set into a grooved frame that is mortised, without nails or lashings, to low-pitched gable roofs.

"There is a single small round hole for an entrance through the thick front wall formed of a solid plank. The entry is well above ground level. This small passage lends protection from attack, as only one man or beast may enter at a time. One descends steps to the interior floor into an open room. There is a large square fire pit lined with rocks or gravel in the center. This is the main source of light and heat. It is the place where all the cooking is done. Along the four sides is a four-foot-wide bench. Partitioned sleeping quarters are outside of the bench, along the walls.

"There is no furniture in the houses other than mortised wooden boxes, some waterproof, that serve as seats as well as storage. Water is stored in wooden boxes with solid bottoms and bentwood sides. A small box containing urine is kept just inside the entry for washing and as a mordant for dyes. Food is served in dishes set on the wooden floor. Boxes and baskets are used for boiling. Roasting is done on spits. There are wooden dishes, platters, bowls, dippers, and spoons. Some spoons are made of horn. Mortars and pestles are made of stone, and large stone slabs are used for grinding and preparing food, medicine, tobacco, and paint. Small, precious, or hazardous items are placed in bags or boxes and hoisted to the ceiling out of reach of the children.

"From their implements and artwork it is obvious that the Tlingit are expert stone carvers, copper workers, wood workers, weavers, and basket makers. The art itself reveals sophistication, restraint, dignity, and elegance.

"Although there is no written language, the Tlingit have an elaborate oral tradition and use totem poles as monuments and reminders. The poles contain crests. The sequence and posture of the crests represent an inscription that reminds the knowledgeable viewer of the story at a glance. It is viewed from the bottom up. The story is told at potlatches, explaining the meaning of the crests and their order of occurrence. The crests are not only objects of art but mythological symbols expressing the past historical and supernatural occurrences upon which claims to lineage and sib status are based.

"The extraordinary event called a potlatch is a large social gathering. Every member of the community plays a role. Potlatches are usually given upon the erection of a new house, marriage, victory in battle, or death. They celebrate the dead with re-incarnation and feast the renewal of the living. The social status of the family, household, or clan is defined and enriched by the amount of wealth given to others. This appears to be a method for redistribution of accumulated wealth, although repayment with interest, at some future date, is expected and places a great burden on some. These elaborate and lengthy parties include singing, dancing, and storytelling. Each group of invited guests competes with the others, sometimes to the point of hostility."

Lisianski also described the people:

"The Kolosh men are of middling stature, have a youthful appearance, and are active and clever. Their hair is lank, strong, and of jet-black color; the face round, the lips thick, and the complexion dark, or copper-color. Both the men and women paint their faces and powder their hair with eagle's down. In war, the men wear a coat of armor. It is usually a heavy walrus hide covered with slabs of ivory from the walrus tusks tightly woven with sinew, and strong enough to deflect a musket ball at close range.

"In the summer they wear very little. In cold season, they wear dresses of fine wool from the wild mountain sheep, embroidered with square figures and fringed with black and yellow tassels. These garments are frequently trimmed and lined with the fur of the sea otter and are very handsome.

"Though the Sitca people are brave, they are extremely cruel to their prisoners, whom they torture to death, or consign to hard labor for life. Europeans receive no mercy at all; men, women, and children will fall upon the poor wretch, at once gashing his flesh, pinching, and burning. They cut off an arm or leg. Others scalp the head while the prisoner is still alive. They cut off the head and throw it away or stick it on a pole.

"On seeing their fine carving of masks, sculptures, domestic utensils, bentwood boxes of inlaid wood, and waterproof baskets, one might suppose these productions the work of a people greatly advanced in civilization."

Lisianski said of the Kolosh women: "Some of the women and girls who live with the Promishliniki have complexions as fair as many Europeans when their skin is cleaned and purified of dirt. Their features are by no means unpleasing. There are men here living with men and supplying the place of women. They are called shupans and are brought up from infancy with the females. They are taught feminine arts and even assume the manner and dress of women so nearly that a stranger would naturally take them for what they are not. This odious practice is so prevalent that the residence of one of these monsters in a house is considered fortunate."

Lisianski also commented that the inflected language of the Tlingit was extremely complex: "Without an alphabet it is difficult to analyze. The word order is reversed. And even within the reversed order, the verbs and nouns did not follow the usual sequence. It is not possible to translate word for word from one to the other."

He noted that both Tlingit and Russian were more flexible in word order than English. He also observed that the Tlingit verbs, unlike English verbs, did not involve time; they stressed the action.

The emphasis was on the completion or the start of an action, much like Russian's imperfective and perfect verb system.

"Tlingit, like Russian and English, to a lesser extent, uses a system of stems," he wrote. "Prefixes, sometimes as many as twelve, are added to the stem, or root. Suffixes are also employed. Some Tlingit words have two functions. They may have independent meaning, or no meaning at all, but merely mark the beginning or ending of a phrase. They may simply be oral literary devices used to create aesthetic distance.

"The sound system of the language includes sounds that are not found in Europe, Asia, or Africa. It is a complex tone language. Phonemic tones are used much as those that occur in Chinese. The difference between words depends on tone. Tone and vowel length changes are dependent upon the grammar required by the meaning intended. There are about twenty-four sounds that are not found in English or Russian.

"There is a system of long, short, and 'clipped' vowels. The 'k,' 'g,' and 'x' sounds may be made with the lips rounded. Such a sound could occur at the beginning, middle, or even ending of a word. There were many uvular sounds made deep in the back of the throat. There were also fricative sounds that allow the air to scrape in a steady stream as it is expelled. One hears stops and even pinching sounds that the Kolosh make by cutting off the airflow in the throat as opposed to the lips. These sounds are pronounced with the air left in the mouth after the throat has cut off the air from the lungs. Many of these sounds are not heard in any other language. In fact, some of them are so subtle, that the foreigner may not hear them at all.

"There are four sounds for something akin to the English 'k' and 'x.' Any one of these sounds may be subjected to a backing, rounding, or pinching, in one, two, or three combinations. The sound system of the Tlingit is one of the most complicated sound systems in the world. That complexity evidences sophistication and intellect in the minds of its speakers. That complexity is reflected in their detailed and intricate art, their houses, and their hopelessly Byzantine social structure. They are an extremely intelligent people whose life of relative ease has afforded them the time to develop complicated systems in every aspect of their lives. Interestingly, they are a ferocious people continually fighting with other tribes and even among themselves. If it comes to war, they will be worthy adversaries."

CHAPTER THIRTEEN

Escape

Clang! Clang! intruded on the morning's silence. Another day began at Atka. Aataagliga ignored the bell and snuggled up to Kakuas-Geti. It had been some time since he had been required to work for the Promishliniki. For an equally long time, Yaskadut had been such an oddity that the Company did not press him into service. Now, in his fourth year, he was accepted by the Aleut as a superior hunter and even as the sire of Kua's son.

Yaskadut had proven his skill with the single-hatch baidarka. One day, Aataagliga, Yaskadut, and four others were hunting along the coast. Yaskadut paddled just outside the surf line along a great cliff. Mountainous Pacific rollers broke against the base of the cliff. Yaskadut noticed a solitary rock sitting at the base of the cliff. The waves just crested the rock, rolled on, and dashed against the cliff. He suddenly turned and caught a wave surfing for the rock.

Aataagliga yelled, "Stop! You will be crushed! You crazy?"

He turned and drove after Yaskadut, paddling hard with his powerful shoulders and arms, but it was too late. He could only fall off the wave and watch with the others. Yaskadut surfed in on the face of the wave. It peaked, breaking just over the top of the rock, depositing the baidarka. Yaskadut spun it around, raised his paddle in triumph, and plunged down the backside of the breaking wave, paddling free of the surf. It was a foolish but dazzling display. The young hunters cheered and waved their paddles in salute. Aataagliga, panting wildly, paddled up to Yaskadut. "You are a fool! Do you want to die?"

"Aataagliga, old friend, sometimes you must do a foolish thing to feel alive."

Yaskadut's skill with the baidarka became a legend, but it cost him his freedom. When the Russians learned of his ability, he was forced to answer the clamor of the bell. He was ordered to hunt along with the others.

He was away on a hunt when the new Company commander established control. Under the regime of the new commander, Zhestokin, everyone—men, women, boys, and girls—was to work for the Company, regardless of age. They all assembled for the roll call, except Aataagliga and Kakuas-Geti. Zhestokin personally called the first roll. He noted their absence.

"Where are those two?" he demanded of the sergeant.

"They are so old that they were not required to work, sir."

"Who said so?"

"The former commander, sir."

"But you have informed all of the Kolosh that there is a new commandant with new rules as I instructed, correct?"

"Sir! Yes, sir!"

"Then they know they are required to report?"

"Sir, everyone has been informed of the rules as instructed," he lied.

"Fetch them at once! Ivanovich, bring the knout. We must set an example, right now."

Ivanovich was an immense brute. He had been sentenced to Siberia for beating his neighbor to death with his fists during a drunken rage. He was selected to join the Promishliniki because of his massive size and strength. His eyes were set deep in high cheek-bones. He had a large, low brow, a wispy beard, and lank hair.

He enjoyed using the gruesome knout, a whip of leather thongs entwined with wire specially designed for flogging. It was frequently used in Siberia to punish prisoners. Ivanovich had known its dreadful caress. He now used it with relish on the miscreants, Aataagliga and Kakuas-Geti, beating them mercilessly before the assembled village.

Enraged, Kua attacked Ivanovich with a hunting knife. He succeeded in stopping the beating—at great cost. A hole was dug to the height of his chin. He was bound and placed in the water-filled hole, then left standing in the hole until the water froze. The assembled village watched Zhestokin boot Kua's head off. It was all for naught. Aataagliga never completely recovered. Kakuas-Geti was carried to her deathbed.

When Yaskadut and the men returned from a forced hunt, there was much talk about avenging the beatings and murders. Many wanted to fight.

In the spring, Zhestokin left the island with the store of furs for Canton. His second in command, Ivan Ivanovich, was a common drunk. The Promishliniki, an undisciplined lot of hunters and opportunists, went on a binge.

Soon Ivanovich learned of a plot among the Kolosh. His interrogators employed beatings, torture, and the threat of rape in an attempt to learn the identity of the ringleaders. The breaking point came when the Promishliniki decided to amuse themselves by lining up Kolosh, one behind the other, and firing their flintlocks through the bodies. They made bets on which weapon would penetrate more bodies.

That night Yaskadut led the Aleut out of the village. They gathered on the brow of a massive rock at the far side of the island. The megalith stood just offshore, separated from the island by the jaws of a narrow, deep ravine. The sky was overcast. At the darkest time of the night, the people lit fires on the lip of the chasm. It appeared that the land continued to slope down to the rock.

The Promishliniki soon discovered that the villagers had gone. In a stuporous rage they pursued. As they approached, they heard the people loudly beating drums and singing their death songs. They charged down the tongue of land toward the rock. Blinded by the fires, many plunged to their deaths in the darkness.

Those who survived sobered and waited for dawn. At dawn, they began shooting the people from across the ravine. One by one the people fell. Once again, it became a game for the Russians.

Soon there were no more easy targets. The Promishliniki advanced on the refuge. Aataagliga, who still suffered from his beating, was wounded in the shoulder by a musket ball. Seeing all the people either dead or dying, he beckoned Yaskadut, and the two slipped into the concealed entrance to his secret cave.

The Promishliniki saw them disappear as if into the rock. Their search finally revealed the entrance, but only one man could enter at a time. Aataagliga and Yaskadut waited just inside on a ledge above the entry. Yaskadut plunged a whaling lance into the neck of the first man who tried to enter.

"Quick!" Aataagliga said. "You get *Ptichka*."

"But it's still high tide."

"Doesn't matter. Wear gut frock, turn baidarka upside down, and push out under water."

"We can't leave. If we step away from the entrance, they will get in."

"Do it! Shoulder broken. I can't do it. You do it!"

Another Promishlinik pushed his way inside the cave. Aataagliga, now without weapons, leapt from his ledge, striking the Russian in the back with both feet. They fell to their deaths on the rocks below.

Yaskadut scrambled for the baidarka. The tide was still too high in the tunnel for the baidarka and his body to pass in an upright position. He pulled the drawstring of the gut frock tight around his chest, just below his armpits, and made sure the frock was pulled watertight around the coaming of the hatch. He took three deep breaths and rolled the baidarka over, ducking underneath, and pushed frantically along the sides of the tunnel, propelling the baidarka, upside down, toward the sea. The water was ice cold. He fought not to gasp as his hands tore at the rock walls. His lungs burned, and he began to black out.

The baidarka popped free into the open sea. Yaskadut released the paddle from its lashings, swiveled his hips, and pushed down against the water with the paddle, rolling upright. He gulped air, slapped the water with the flat of the paddle blade to stop the roll, and dug for the open sea and freedom.

The Promishliniki caught sight of him. A yell went up as they ran to the cliff's edge. Shots rang out. Within minutes, Yaskadut was pulling hard to sea beyond the range of the muskets.

The Russians ran to the village and put out to sea in pursuit, but the weather was threatening and they did not persist. An Aleut in their lead baidarka stopped paddling and glanced at the sky. He watched Yaskadut disappear in the rising seas and drifted, looking at the mountaintops and the clouds, as a companion arrived.

"That one heads into bad weather."

"Sun's rays suck up the ocean like the fingers of the octopus. Soon there will be wind and rain. He will die."

"Maybe not. Maybe he gave his daughter to the North Wind." They laughed.

Yaskadut paddled toward the weather cauldron that was the Gulf of Alaska. Headwinds and countercurrents could defeat him. He would leave Atka behind and paddle eastward, south of Amila, Seguan, Island of Four Mountains, Umnak, Unalaska, Unimak, Shumagin, and along the Alaska Peninsula with the Aleutian mountain range peaking over the horizon to guide him.

He fell to the south, knowing that the west winds would back to the east. They would strengthen and blow from starboard, driving him northward toward the coast of the mainland. With a following swell and quartering wind waves, he could ride the current while the sea temperature warmed his way home. He knew that after the Aleutians, he could coast, but he must avoid being driven upon a lea shore by the high swells and breaking seas into the hands of the enemy.

Frequently, he stopped, spat into the water, and watched his spittle drift. He placed his hand in the water to feel the temperature. He could feel changes of wind temperature on his earlobes. He looked for birds and fish that favored warmer water. He observed the drift of storm-damaged kelp. He noted subtle changes in the color of the sea and sky. At night, he could see the loom of reflected starlight above shore snow. In daylight, he watched cloud masses clinging to island and coastal mountains. He stayed within the range of cormorants, kittiwakes, and pigeon guillemot, knowing they would be near land.

He knew the secrets of steering by swells in the open sea. He ignored temporary waves created by local winds as they crested and broke. The long slow swells, born in the northeast, rose and fell as they rolled to the southwest along the Aleutians and down the coast of Alaska. Long ago he had learned to select the persistent patterns. He could follow them even in the night or overcast. The sun and stars, when visible, provided corroboration and course correction in stormy and confused seas.

With his genitals on the sole of the baidarka, he could feel the surface waves reflected from islands and the shoreline. He found the great warm Kuroshio Current that swept up the coast of Japan, along Kamchatka, and across the top of the North Pacific, flanking the Aleutian Islands before branching south into the California Current. He sought this two-knot current and following seas. Without them, he could never paddle and drift the 1,640 miles home.

Onward he pushed, with finwhales, humpback, beluga, and porpoise. He saw sea lion, ringed seal, Arctic tern, and sea gulls. He knew their migration routes. Into the night, he drove. On clear, crisp nights, he kept the northern star off his left shoulder, at about sixty degrees, as he paddled toward dawn—a yellow radiance in a pale sky. On he pressed, in the company of cavorting orcas. *Ptichka* was one with the following sea and current.

As the sun rose, Yaskadut felt the breeze against his back. Tears welled with gratitude and thoughts of Shee Atiká Sound. He had grown to manhood among strangers. He thought of the Koniag, the Chugach, and the Aleut. He would always be grateful to Kuimariaq and Aataagliga. They were also his fathers. He spoke their names aloud, thanked them, and wished them well in the land of the Milky Way. A lone albatross drifted overhead, due east, leading him home.

He was free, traveling in a magic baidarka on a beautiful and bountiful sea. At night, Yaskadut listened to the singing of the whales and the blowing of the dolphin. Thanks to his mentors, he would not just survive in this environment, but thrive. The weather was not his enemy. He knew its moods. If a great storm came, he could perish. If he drowned, it was because he had ignored or misunderstood Tlam-Shua, the inscrutable force that speaks through gales and storms at sea. If he drowned, the otter people would take him.

Man was his enemy. Yaskadut had to follow the coast for food and shelter from storms, but he had to avoid his fellow creature. He must stay just beyond the normal hunting range of that predator.

As evening fell he heard a pod of orcas racing past his baidarka, followed by humpback, dolphin, seals, and sea lions in great numbers. The sea was alive with terrified animals, overtaking him, passing him, and rushing on. An apocalyptic rumble sounded far behind him. He turned to face it. A massive explosion lit the western horizon in the predawn light. Pieces of glowing magma shot into the sky. An eerie glow reflected off low overhead clouds. Lightning crackled and laced towering ash-choked rain clouds as thunder reverberated.

Yaskadut braced for the tsunami that would follow. A cresting rogue wave rose above him. He drove *Ptichka* directly into it to gain height, abruptly turned abeam, and stuck his paddle into its glistening green wall as he surfed down and across its face below a roaring waterfall. As it dissipated, an immense swell swept beneath *Ptichka*, lifting them up to see great plumes of black smoke and gray steam. An island rose from the sea in the infernal light. Yaskadut watched in awe while dawn turned to midday. Again, he took up the paddle.

He ate raw fish and crustaceans picked off kelp. When no rain fell, he was driven ashore to look for water. On such occasions, he risked a small fire to cook game. He never slept on land. He anchored his baidarka to kelp. Alert to the slightest wind shift, swing of the boat, or noise, he slept with the otter.

In good weather, the rhythm of sunrise, sunset, daylight, and dark harmonized with scudding clouds and turning stars. Always the rise and fall of the following sea carried him home. His mind cleared as he recalled his mother, Tle'an, his uncle Qa-tla, his grandfather and grandmother, Galweit and Gaelgix.

He remembered how Kua had died. Names of childhood friends, enemies, and long-forgotten nursery rhymes, songs, and dances recurred. Scents of flowers, food, home, and hearth were strong. He traveled to his favorite mountain and lay among the stunted wildflowers, lichen, and moss, with Xietl drifting overhead. He thought of "tooth," his father's hunting spear, and compared it to the iron lance of Aataagliga that lay lashed to the deck of *Ptichka*. The foul insult "gaxtan" came to mind, and he wondered how his old enemy YaKwáan would react to him.

Tl'anaxe'eda'kwaa appeared. He admired her cool beauty as a lover would. In awe of her wisdom, he held conversations with her. She reminded him,

> "The song bird lives.
> The sea otter shall not die.
> The salmon are prolific.
> This warrior and his people shall not perish."

He drifted and paddled through reveries of the past and day-dreams of the future. He became the rise and fall of the sea from dawn until dusk and through the night.

Storms crept up in the dark. The wind built and seas grew. Horrifying waves tossed *Ptichka*, breaking over her, rolling her, and even pitching her end over end, but she remained afloat on the surface, as light and safe as a storm petrel. He need only cling to her and stay with her. This gift of Aataagliga was a magical thing of beauty. He stroked her lines with tenderness and admiration.

With each day and night he became more a creature of the sea. He did not miss man or conversation. He became accustomed to raw fish. His hands hardened and callused with the seawater and constant paddling. His lean torso and arms became stone. His face weathered as salt collected in his eyebrows, ears, hair, and thin mustache. His sight became more acute over great distances. He became accustomed to the sea. It was his home. This was his existence. He was a sea creature. On he paddled. It seemed he had never done anything else.

In the evening, as he passed far out to sea, south of Kodiak, he heard the wailing of lost souls. Women and children cried. Men shouted in anguish. The smell of death insulted his nostrils. He passed an evil place.

Schelikov had massacred most of the Aleuts on the island in 1773. The spirits of the people still lingered there. Yaskadut saw their terrible story in a vision:

The people had never seen a European. The arrival of these aliens was presaged by a solar eclipse two days earlier.

The Aleuts fled in terror to a rock outcropping accessible only at low tide by a gravel spit.

One of their members betrayed the secret. Schelikov's Promishliniki pushed a four-hundred-pound cannon out onto the spit at low tide and swept the rock with grapeshot. The terrified people had never seen a firearm.

Promishliniki overran the outcropping with muskets, bayonets, and cutlasses. Many people, in sheer terror, plunged to their deaths off the seaward cliff of the rock.

Yaskadut saw the horror, mayhem, and murder. He heard their dead souls and trembled in anger, dismay, and revulsion. He did not know why he saw and heard these things. *This is, was, and will be an evil place forever*, he thought.

Many years before Yaskadut's passage, Schelikov had written, "We had a great battle on our hands, which we won with the help of God."

Yaskadut pressed on across the Gulf of Alaska, leaving the land of Aataagliga the Aleut, past the land of Kuimariaq the Chugach, and beyond the land of the Koniag. He saw the face of Yaskadut the Bear Slayer. Visions of these three men blended into one. They had molded his character and imparted their wisdom. In him, they were embodied, and the wisdom passed on.

Now he was forced to paddle against the Alaska current that swept up the coast to the north, turning west along the Alaska Peninsula. The westerly winds swirled northward as they struck the coast. He paddled against the current and winds, following the coastline as he turned south. Close ashore the going was easier, but he risked capture. He wore the dress of the Aleut. His weapons were Aleut. Tlingits would attack on sight.

He was less wary at night. He closed with the shore and listened to the sound of the surf, feeling the waves rebound from the rocky coast.

The sea, the land, even the smell of the wind grew more familiar as he approached his home. Memories of childhood flooded his mind, only to be replaced by plans for the future. *The Tlingit will not fall prey. They will not be decimated as the Aleut. They will not disappear as the Eyak, Koniag, and the Chugach. They will resist. Xietl protects us, and Tl'anaxe'eda'kwaa advises.*

With each stroke of the paddle, Yaskadut resolved to fight. He made plans for the enemy. He knew their ways, their language, their weapons, and their iron.

On he drove against the current and the wind. His heart grew light, and joy lent strength to his arms as he approached Shee Atiká.

During his long exile and slavery, he had not allowed himself to think of home and his loved ones. Now ol' Galweit and Gaelgix were on his mind. Did they live, or had they walked into the forest? What of Tle'an? Would Qa-tla, the strong one, be proud of him? Yaskadut, the slayer of bears, lived. X'uts did not kill him, for here he was—Yaskadut the son, who embodied Yaskadut the father. Were Box House, Wolf House, and Eagle's Nest still strong? How many would there be to fight? Would others join them? The Promishliniki would come pursuing the otter people. *We must be ready.*

On and on he paddled, singing Tlingit songs and reciting Tlingit history. Visions, dreams, memories, and songs nourished him and replaced sleep. The thought of Shee Atiká and his beautiful mountain quenched his thirst.

Yaskadut approached the Shee Atiká Sound from seaward. He knew the Tlingit war canoes would intercept him if he dared pass through the inland waterways. As the sun rose, its rays illuminated his favorite mountain—a great snow-capped peak, the cone-shaped beacon that marked the entrance to Shee Atiká Sound. Yaskadut struck boldly for village.

A phalanx of Tlingit baidari formed a battle line to intercept the intruder. Yaskadut feinted toward the south end of the line. Just beyond musket or bow, he turned and stroked at full speed for the center of the line of war canoes.

Yaskadut paddled *Ptichka* in on the following sea at more than twelve knots. She flew with white wings of bow spray, passing within fifty yards of war canoes on either side. A hail of musket balls, arrows, and spears filled the air. The marksmen were startled that Yaskadut drove though the middle of their line toward shore.

They were amazed with *Ptichka*'s speed and were forced to hold fire when he passed among them.

The aroused village ran to the shore with arms at the ready. As Yaskadut surfed his baidarka ashore, there was a collective yell, and the villagers swooped down the gravel beach. An ominous rumble shook the earth. An eagle swooped from on high directly at the crowd, screaming, with talons extended. The earth trembled. The people stopped dead in their tracks.

Finally, ol' Galweit stepped forward and slowly approached Yaskadut, who had not uttered a sound. He hunched his shoulders and peered into the face of Yaskadut. Tears sprang into his eyes.

"Yaskadut, my son, it is thee," he said softly. "Yaskadut! Yaskadut! My son has returned!" he announced, turning to the crowd.

YaḴwáan, now a towering man, dressed as a shaman, slunk into the woods.

Tle'an ran to embrace Yaskadut.

"Have you turned Aleut?" she asked.

"I am Tlingit. Kiks.adi Tlingit of Shee Atiká Sound, in the village of Shee Atiká, House of Eagle's Nest. I shall always be."

It would be tedious to tell each individual of the village his life's story, but it was an important that he share it. He decided to tell them all at once, in a dance before the fire in Eagle's Nest. Many of the members of the house helped him prepare costumes, masks, and props. He composed songs and choreographed his dance. It had to be accurate. That was the way his people preserved their history.

Ol' Galweit held a great potlatch. There was feasting, dancing, and song. Ol' Galweit gave away everything he had in celebration of the return of Yaskadut the son — Yaskadut the grandson. He honored ancestors and relatives with stories of primordial times.

Yaskadut remained hidden during the celebration. When the meal ended he appeared, as if out of the air. He was a young boy wandering through the woods. He lay down to sleep. He suddenly awoke and saw naked men with labrets, nose-bones, and beads hanging from pierced ears. He was taken prisoner on board a baidar, far to the northern land of the Koniag. He was a slave but not abused. He learned of their hunting, fishing, and gathering. He sang their songs and told their stories.

He was traded to the Chugach. Again, he donned masks and costumes to portray the Chugach. He learned to hunt and fish from these people. He hunted seal, sea lion, otter, and even whale from baidarki and baidar.

He became Kuimariaq, and built a baidarka in the Chugach fashion. He went on a great hunt, and was marooned on an ice floe. He slept, froze, and lay dying. Xietl brought Tl'anaxe'eda'kwaa. Yaskadut danced into the sky, beyond the moon and sun, to the Milky Way, where he visited warrior spirits and spoke with Yaskadut, the Bear Slayer. Tl'anaxe'eda'kwaa told him of the future, and warned him of a powerful enemy who would come to kill the otter, the salmon, and the Tlingit. He told the people of her advice and what they must do to resist this enemy.

Yaskadut became Aataagliga, the funny old Aleut with the heart of an ice bear. He spoke Aleut as he crabbed around the fire on bowed legs. The Tlingit laughed until they heard about the Anooshi who came and killed the animals and the people of the Aleutian Islands. Dressed as a Russian, he danced, fired guns, and tortured the Aleut. He fought a battle with Aataagliga at his side. He showed how Aataagliga sacrificed himself to help Yaskadut escape.

He paddled his snow-white baidarka, *Ptichka*, across the great North Pacific. He encountered orca, sea lions, and humpbacks. The fire in the center of Eagle's Nest burst high into the air as he paddled away from a volcano giving birth to an island at sea. Drums rumbled and Eagle's Nest shook.

He evaded the Tlingit war canoes and greeted the people of Shee Atiká. The earth trembled and the people screamed and stamped their feet in terror and joy.

In the half-light of the roaring fire, the people lived the tale. When it was funny, they laughed. When it was sad, they cried. When there was danger, they gasped. In battle, they cheered and mourned as heroes fought and died.

Failings of the props and costumes were ignored. They loved the drama, enjoying it with the freedom and joy of children. They did not see Yaskadut imitating Kuimariaq, Aataagliga, Xietl, Tl'anaxe'eda'kwaa, and the Anooshi. When he dressed as Tl'anaxe'eda'kwaa, painting his naked body green and wearing a seaweed wig, they saw Tl'anaxe'eda'kwaa. When he wore the mask and feathers of Xietl, he became Xietl.

The dance carried on through the night and ended with dawn. When it was over, the people knew that he was a shaman with vast knowledge of strange and foreign people. He knew the past and foresaw the future. He communed with the gods and fought the demons. He could see great distances and feel the presence of the enemy. He had visited the land of the dead and returned. He was given the potlatch name "The Man of Thunder, Son of Xietl."

CHAPTER FOURTEEN

Speech of Skayeutlelt the Elder

In the fall, fifty-eight years after Captain Chirikov's 1741 abortive landing, Baranov left Kodiak with two Russian ships and two hundred baidarki for Shee Atiká. Thirty baidarki, with two hundred Aleuts, were lost in storms. The ships finally anchored in Shee Atiká Sound. A storm drove the baidarki ashore. They landed in pitch dark at the edge of a dense forest. The exhausted men lay where they fell.

A long, high-pitched war cry pierced the forest. It was the Tlingit. Some Aleuts froze, awaiting death; others fled directly into the arms of their tormentors waiting in the woods. Their pitiful cries ladled fear upon the beach. The Promishliniki fired into the dark at hideous screams. At dawn, the Russians broke for the ships, leaving the Aleuts to their baidarki.

The Russians begged Baranov to leave the godforsaken land with its bloody savages. Baranov would not. He dispatched a peace party under a white flag. Baranov led his men ashore in the wind, rain, and sleet. They met a large band of Tlingit. Baranov described them as "the most hideous band of human beings I have ever seen. Some painted their faces black and red in macabre designs. Their hair was full of black grease and red ochre sprinkled with down. They assumed animal disguises with horns and gleaming teeth. They were not human but demons from hell."

The elder Skayeutlelt spoke with Yaskadut on the way to meet Baranov. "I must speak with him," he explained.

"I know this man and the things that his Promishliniki did to the Aleut," Yaskadut replied.

"The Aleuts are cowards."

"And the Eyak, Koniag, and Chugach—were they cowards too?"

"They are old women."

"Baranov leads many and has thousands of slaves. There is a great land across the sea where they are more than the stars. He has guns and iron. He wants slaves. I will never be a slave again. Cut off the head of this beast."

"Yaskadut, you have grown bitter. We should talk. Perhaps we can slow the invasion."

"They are a ravenous tide."

"We will talk."

Baranov was a short, stout man of fifty-four. He sported a black wig tied to his pate with a bandanna. He limped. His arthritic hands curled at his sides after a lifetime of hard work and loyalty to his country and the Company. He watched three battle canoes of the Shee Atiká Kiks.adi approach his camp. They sang as they paddled, stopping short of landing. No Tlingit would enter a stranger's camp without an invitation.

Skayeutlelt stood on a platform that was carved behind the upturned bow of the lead canoe. He delivered a rhythmic and rhetorical speech. The art consisted in repetition of a theme in many different forms:

"We were your enemies—we sought to do you injury.

"You were our enemy—you sought to injure us.

"We wish to be good friends. We would forget the past.

"You say you wish to be good friends. Will you forget the past?

"We no longer wish to molest you; forbear to injure us.

"If you forbear, we will forbear.

"Henceforward, we will be good friends."

The speech continued half an hour. Baranov waited patiently. He knew that elaborate ceremony must be observed. He knew the Tlingit would dance and sing for hours to entertain and impress the Russians.

"Great Chief Skayeutlelt, I come in peace. We want to live here in peace. We need a place and will give you valuable goods for the land where we will build our camp. Will you sell us some land so that we may build a home?"

"Natook. Your name is known. You are a great warrior, but I am no chief. We do not have chiefs and I cannot sell you this land. I do not own the land. No one owns it. Who owns the forest, the sky, the water? No man owns the rivers, streams, and lakes. No one can claim the wind and the clouds. Long ago Yel set the daylight, moon, and stars free."[4]

"But we wish to settle here and stay on this land, to call it home."

"This is where the Tlingit hunt. The Tlingit are only the care-takers of the land. Other people hunt here only with our permission. If you come in peace, you may take what you need. No more. You cannot stay. The rocks, trees, mountains, and streams are alive and free. The animals are our brothers. No one can sell them or the place where they live."

"We also must have a place to live. We want to stay, peace-fully, and enjoy the bounty of the land."

---

4   This speech is inspired by Chief Seattle's beautiful letter of 1852, in response to a U.S. government inquiry about buying tribal lands.

"How many are you?"

"Only a few will stay. The Aleut will return to their land after the hunts."

"That is not good. We have not agreed to let you or the Aleut hunt in this place. You will take more than you need."

"But you said you do not own this land."

"When we are here, the land provides us with our needs so long as we respect it. We will not let others take the animals and plants. When we have enough, we let others hunt, but they must take no more than they need. We are here to protect the land that feeds us. If we move on, someone else will care for it. People come and go but the land abides. The forest remains. The bear, the otter, the salmon thrive. Someday I will be gone, so how can I sell you what remains behind?"

"We also will not be here forever. We too will respect the land and the animals."

"I have heard otherwise. I have heard that you consume the otter people. Why do you take so many otter? Are there so many people in your land that need the warmth? If you kill too many, the otter people will die."

"I promise you that we will be good neighbors to you, the land, and the otter people. You must let us live here."

"Why?"

"Because we can keep others from coming. As many others as there are stars in the sky, all with muskets and cannon, want to come here from many lands."

"We will not sell what is not ours. But some of our people say they will accept your iron axes, hatchets, and knives. They will take the cloth and blankets in trade. My people think they need those things. It is true iron is stronger than wood, bone, copper, or stone.

If the people agree, the Shee Atiká Kiks.adi will live with you as brothers, but you must not bring more. You must leave this place as you found it for our children and their children. You must agree."

"Yes. We will be brothers and care for the forest. I will put this promise in the pictures we call writing and send it to the Tsar of Russia, our great chief. He will sign it and never break the promises I have made to you."

"We do not need the picture writing if you give your word."

"How are promises remembered when you are gone and others take your place?"

"I tell my children and my children tell theirs. As long as there are Shee Atiká Kiks.adi, we will not forget."

"It is our custom to write things down, so there can be no mistake."

"It is dishonor to forget or lie, but you may keep picture writing if you cannot trust your children. It would be good to have strong brothers. I must talk to the people. If they agree, you can stay here and hunt—for a while."

"Great Chief, one among us is a man of God, Father Gideon. He wishes to speak to the people. He was sent to you by the Holy Synod of the Russian Orthodox Church in St. Petersburg, Russia, with the blessing of His Majesty Tsar Alexander."

"We will listen to this man of God."

"Thank you, Honorable Skayeutlelt, and I thank the people for allowing me to speak," said Father Gideon.

"I come in peace in the name of God to share the story of the creation of the world. Listen to the word of God and gain life everlasting. Listen and ye shall find peace. Out of the watery abyss, God created heaven and divided the waters into seas by land called Earth. And the earth brought forth grass, herbs, and fruit.

"Out of the void, God created two great lights: the greater light to rule the day, the moon and stars to brighten the night, and God saw that it was good. And there was evening and morning.

"God said, 'Let the waters swarm with living creatures, and let birds fly above the earth in the heavens.' And God created the great sea monsters and every living creature that moveth. God saw that it was good. And God blessed them, saying, 'Be fruitful, and multiply.'

"And God said, 'Let us make man in our image, after our like-ness: and let them have dominion over the fish of the sea, and over the birds of the heavens.' And God created man in his image. And God saw everything that he had made, and, behold, it was very good.

"The first man and woman of this earth lived in a beautiful garden. There was neither hunger nor cold. The man was Adam and the woman was Eve. They desired more. They wanted knowl-edge of good and evil, like gods. They disobeyed God and ate fruit from the tree of knowledge. God drove them from the garden. Man was forced to earn a living by the sweat of his brow. Man came to know death.

"Man did multiply and thrive, but murder, rape, and plunder filled the land. A pagan world was ruled by dread, and sudden justice struck with sword or spear. God caused a great flood to cleanse the earth. He spared the only good man left on earth with his family. They survived and peopled the world, but it was still man's lot to live and die in sin.

"Once again God took pity on man. He sired a son of a blessed virgin. This son was called Jesus. Jesus was sent among the people to teach the will of God. Once a great multitude of people gathered upon a mount and Jesus taught them, saying:

"'Blessed are the poor in spirit; for theirs is the kingdom of heaven.

"'Blessed are they that mourn: for they shall be comforted.

"'Blessed are the meek: for they shall inherit the earth.

"'Blessed are they that hunger and thirst after righteousness: for they shall be filled.

"'Blessed are the merciful: for they shall obtain mercy.

"'Blessed are the pure in heart: for they shall see God.

"'Blessed are the peacemakers: for they shall be called sons of God.'

"If you are worthy, you will be spared everlasting torment in hell. To be worthy, you must not indulge anger. You must love your enemies, and pray for them that persecute you. According to the ancient Code of Hammurabi, 'an eye for an eye, and a tooth for a tooth' was just, but that old world and that old creed are dead.

"Jesus said, 'Whosoever smiteth thee on thy right cheek, turn to him the other also.' Jesus was betrayed as an enemy of the state and crucified. The son of God's tears and blood washed away original sin so that you could be saved and enter the Kingdom of Heaven. God, the All-Powerful, the Omniscient, the Omnipotent, did not forsake Jesus. God, the Father, gave his only begotten son to atone for original sin. But Jesus rose in spiritual victory over death through the acceptance of death. 'As in Adam all die, so also in Christ shall all be made alive.'

"If you listen to these revelations and believe in them, you will not perish but have life everlasting in the Kingdom of God. This is the word of God who created the world and everything in it. Believe it. Embrace it and all pain in this veil of tears will fall away. You will be joyous and prosper here and now. You will attain immortal bliss in the hereafter. Merely ask, and it shall be given you; seek, and ye shall find; knock, and it shall be opened unto you. Love, sacrifice, and redemption are the essence of Christianity.

"If you ignore this plea and harden your heart to the Lord God, you will be cast into an everlasting inferno. At the end of time, when God's judgment is held, seven angels will loose hell's torments upon those who do not believe. Seven angels will blast seven trumpets, and the plagues of hail, fire, and blood will be cast upon the earth. With the blast of a trumpet, a great star will fall from heaven, and the fountains and streams and waters will become as bitter and poisonous as wormwood, and men will die. Even the sun, moon, and stars will grow dim. The pit of the abyss will open. Smoke will rise from a great furnace, darkening the sun and the air. Out of the smoke will appear locusts with the sting of scorpions, the bodies of warhorses, golden crowns, and iron breastplates.

"They will have faces of men and hair of women. Their teeth will be the teeth of lions. The Angel of the Abyss will torment non-believers with such venom that they will beg for death and oblivion, in vain. This scourge will continue day and night.

"Angels of death riding horses with lion heads, tails of serpents, and breastplates of fire, smoke, and brimstone shall slay mankind for his murders, sorceries, fornication, and theft.

"With the seventh trumpet will come the time of the dead to be judged. Lightning, thunder, and earthquakes will be followed by deadly hail. The Great Dragon will be cast out of heaven and come to earth. This Prince of Darkness, this Satan, will war on the sons of men. This devil will come out of the sea with ten horns and seven heads, with the body of a leopard and the feet of a bear. He will pursue the souls of men and devour them. The birds of the firmament shall eat the flesh of commoner and king, the flesh of all men both free and bond, and great and small.

"After the great battle in heaven and on earth, the angels of God will seize Mephistopheles. This Satan, this God of Hades, will be bound in hell for a thousand years but will rise again only to be cast into a lake of fire and brimstone, where he and all nonbelievers shall burn forever and ever.

"Listen to me and open your hearts. Embrace life and truth. Abandon your evil ways and step into the light of God. Turn away from eternal hell. May the blood of Christ wash away your sins. I leave you with this beautiful gift. A prayer to Our Lord God that will bring you comfort and strength throughout your life:

"The Lord is my shepherd;

"I shall not want.

"He maketh me to lie down in green pastures;

"He leadeth me beside still waters.

"He restoreth my soul:

"He guideth me in the paths of righteousness for his name's sake.

"Yea, though I walk through the valley of the shadow of death,

"I will fear no evil; for thou art with me:

"Thy rod and thy staff, they comfort me.

"Thou preparest a table before me in the presence of mine enemies;

"Thou hast anointed my head with oil;

"My cup runneth over.

"Surely goodness and loving kindness shall follow me all the days of my life;

"And I shall dwell in the house of the Lord forever.

"Amen.

"I come as a friend seeking to save your souls and will not leave this land without an answer from the people of Shee Atiká. Please consider these words as a gift of truth and life. I await a reply from my red brothers. When you reply, know that we wish you to speak freely."

Yaskadut said nothing. He remembered the Koniag, the Chugach, and the Aleut. The proffered goods were examined. Baranov extended his hand. The elder Skayeutlelt took it. He, Yaskadut, and fifty warriors turned to their war canoes and paddled out to sea.

CHAPTER FIFTEEN

War and Desecration

"Why should we let these witches live in our midst?" asked Yaskadut.

"We will let the people decide. We will have a great talk and then decide," replied Skayeutlelt.

Yaskadut reminded the him of all the killing, torture, abuse, and exploitation he had seen. He explained, once again, how the Russians killed some and seduced others.

"Yaskadut, the Bear Slayer, son of Yaskadut the Bear Slayer, you are a wise man. You have traveled far and seen much. I value your wisdom and judgment, but we must let the people decide," replied Skayeutlelt.

There was a great debate among the people. The elder Skayeutlelt urged peace and accommodation. Yaskadut urged war as preferable to annihilating assimilation. He was acutely aware of the dilemma. Either war or assimilation could lead to extinction. YaKwáan spoke for many of the people who wanted the Russians' goods. Some were greatly disturbed and moved by the talk of Father Gideon.

The next day, several Tlingit made trades and accepted gifts. The Tlingit gathered at the site of the meeting and began dancing and singing. They wore feathers, masks, and special dancing regalia.

The leaders carried battle wands decorated with two-dimensional designs on either side. They were used to signal warriors' movements in combat. Here they were used as a conductor uses a baton to coordinate complex and sinuous movements of the dancers. With each change of position of the paddles, members of the dancing team executed maneuvers in perfect coordination and timing.

They told stories of hunting, battle, and a great migration of the people. Some dances were violent, others merely slow movement of shoulders and hips on unmoving feet. At times, all of the dancers shook intricately carved raven rattles featuring interlocked figures of animals and grotesque men. Box drums of red cedar with engraved figures on the sides were beaten with fists, accentuating the chanting and songs. The songs ranged from mournful to fierce.

Rival groups of dancers watched one another, seeking a mistake that they could mock. At times, the threatening rivalry made the audience uncomfortable.

Baranov's Russians sang and his Aleuts danced. Competition developed. Each dance and each song belonged to a particular person or group and could not be repeated by others without permission.

Yaskadut did not attend. He went alone through the woods to his boyhood mountain. He remained there without food or water for five days. Tl'anaxe'eda'kwaa came. She reminded him to protect the people—all the people. Warriors would die, but the people must survive, and that meant war. He was told that he had to rouse the people.

Yaskadut returned to the village. He waited for old Skayeutlelt, whom he loved like a father, to go to the bathhouse late at night. It was the old man's habit to bathe alone. Yaskadut crept into the bathhouse. With tears in his eyes, he cut the old man's throat. He drove a

Russian dagger with double eagles on the handle into the old man's heart. He left it there.

When the people discovered Skayeutlelt's body and the Russian dagger, Yaskadut had to restrain them to prevent an immediate attack. He counseled patience and cunning while assuring them of an eventual victory.

YaḴwáan screamed in pain and hatred for an immediate attack upon his recent benefactors. Yaskadut reminded the people that YaḴwáan had urged acceptance of the Russians and their goods but now demanded a suicidal attack upon them. Yaskadut's cunning won more allies than YaḴwáan's emotion.

Baranov built a fort on Shee Atiká Sound. It was christened Fort St. Michael. Barracks, storehouses, and quarters for the commanding officer were constructed. A bathhouse was erected. The compound was surrounded by a stockade strengthened with blockhouses. The Russians did not trust the people they called "Kolosh." The Tlingit in turn did not trust the Russky, but just as Baranov promised, most of the Aleuts left and returned to Kodiak.

With the passage of time, the Russians began to despoil the land. They slaughtered the otter people. They treated the Tlingit like slaves, plied them with liquor, seduced and raped the women. Yaskadut's prophecy proved correct.

Yaskadut spent most of his time alone. He traveled up and down the coast of Alaska in *Ptichka*. A mysterious figure, he disappeared and reappeared in such distant places so rapidly that some believed he was a witch and *Ptichka* could fly. He was suspected of leading a massacre of Russians at Ilyama Bay, north of Shee Atiká. The Tlingit in the vicinity feigned ignorance. Rumors spread of a shaman in a bewitched qayaq bringing death to the Russian Promishliniki.

A Russian outpost at Yakutat was overrun, and all the Russians and Aleuts were put to death. There were whispers of a pending attack on the redoubt at Fort St. Michael, but the Kiks.adi of Shee Atiká appeared friendly. Some Kolosh women lived with the Promishliniki in the garrison.

Fort St. Michael received reports of Russian leadership abuse and consequent disorder in Kodiak. Promishliniki and Aleut alike made perilous baidarka journeys to Shee Atiká to inform Baranov and plead for his immediate intervention. Finally, in June of 1802, Baranov took most of the soldiers and hunters on an inspection tour of Kodiak. He left behind a garrison of sixty Promishliniki and two hundred Aleuts.

The Tlingit women in residence had been reporting the habits of the garrison to Yaskadut. While Baranov was away, a Russian holiday was celebrated. The Tlingit knew that almost everyone in the fort would be drunk by midnight.

Lieutenant Shchegolyanin, a dandy and a drunk, had been left in command. He maintained a liaison with a schopan from the village; Shchegolyanin preferred the male schopan to the native women and frequently allowed him to enter through the church built into the wall of the stockade. There was a back door from the settlement below the fort to allow the Kolosh to enter for services. The front door faced the compound of the stockade, providing access for the Russians. Over time, the schopan acquired access free of scrutiny through the empty church.

Yaskadut knew of those meetings. While the Russians celebrated, he slew the schopan and put on his clothing. He passed through the church, crossed the compound, and entered Shchegolyanin's quarters. Shchegolyanin was drunk and did not notice or did not care. He quietly opened the door. Yaskadut entered.

When the attack commenced, a young Russian ran to the lieutenant's quarters. He was shocked to find Shchegolyanin on his knees with his trousers around his ankles. His throat was slit from ear to ear.

The Kiks.adi burst from the forest in war paint, masks, and armor. A fleet of war canoes surrounded the redoubt. Warriors swarmed up the steep bank in the foggy night. At the first sound of battle, Tlingit women inside the redoubt stabbed their lovers, then set fire to the stockade and powder magazine.

Confusion and darkness added to the terror of the night attack by Tlingit in armor and helmets with grotesque masks. Resistance was feeble and disorganized.

Yaskadut commanded the attack from a nearby hillside. The Russians were burned out of the fortifications and forced to leap from the blockhouses to their deaths on the spears of the Kiks.adi waiting below, who shrieked with delight. Those who did not die immediately were tortured to death. The few surviving women were raped and their children taken as slaves. Some Aleut escaped in their baidarki to ships of English and American traders in the bay.

Captain John Ebbets, on the American ship *Alert*, paid ransom for some of the captives and took them aboard his ship.

The Tlingit called Americans "Boston Men" and the English "King George Men." A King George man, Captain Henry Barber of the ship *Unicorn*, feigned a desire to continue trade with the Tlingit. When Yaskadut sent his oldest nephew to trade otter pelts for muskets, the young man was clapped in irons. Captain Barber threatened to hang the young man if the remaining captives and otter pelts stored at the redoubt were not brought aboard his ship.

Captain Barber appeared the great hero. He volunteered to take the other ransomed captives aboard his ship. Once aboard, he took them all to Kodiak. There he demanded a ransom of fifty thousand rubles from Baranov for those he rescued as well as those he had gained in a trade for Yaskadut's nephew.

After considerable dickering, Baranov paid ten thousand rubles. Captain Barber was known thereafter among the Tlingit as "Lukciyan Kutici-yadi," which meant "child of a mink's scent glands."

Captain Barber sailed to Canton and exchanged his ill-gotten furs for teas, silks, nankeens, chinaware, and gold. He was arrogant enough to return to Shee Atiká in August of 1803.

The Kiks.adi, led by Yaskadut, greeted Captain Barber and opened trade. On the second day, Yaskadut came aboard from a baidar laden with otter pelts. The ship's crew were engaged in repairing sail, running shot in the armorer's forge, spinning yarn, making sinnet, and otherwise pursuing ship's maintenance.

Canoes gathered alongside. Yaskadut stood by, casually leaning on the rail, looking down into a baidar laden with pelts. He beckoned to the captain to come and inspect them. When Captain Barber leaned over the rail to view the pelts, Yaskadut yanked his coat up over his head, stabbed him in the back, and threw him overboard. Kiks.adi, armed with daggers, pistols, and pikes, flooded the main deck. Of the twenty-three hands on board, ten were killed and nine wounded.

The cook fought back with boiling water. They butchered him with an ax. The chief mate, although shot through the body, retrieved a musket and rallied the other three able-bodied crewmen. They fired muskets through loopholes in the break of the forecastle. Finally, they were able to bring a swivel gun, loaded with canister of shot, to bear. One round painted the main deck red. Blood ran out the scuppers.

The Kiks.adi in the baidar tried to cut the bow cable. They planned to tow the ship aground by the stern anchor line. A blast of the swivel gun turned the baidar into a bucket of blood. The crew plunged their jack knives into the skulls of the Kiks.adi that survived, slipped the anchor, and limped out to sea. The Kiks.adi, having suffered grievous losses, slipped away into the woods.

Baranov sailed back to Shee Atiká with a fleet of ships in the summer of 1804. They were the *Aleksander*, of one hundred tons and a crew of thirty-eight; the eighty-ton *Ekaterina*, with a crew of twenty; the sixty-ton *Yermak*, crewed by fifteen; and the forty-five-ton *Rostislav*, with a crew of twelve.

The ships were accompanied by two hundred and sixty baidarki manned by over five hundred Aleuts armed with English flintlock muskets. Baranov left a message for Captain Lisianski, urging the *Neva* to join his forces in Shee Atiká for a united attack on the Kolosh. It was his intention to lead a punitive expedition against the Kiks.adi of Shee Atiká, rebuild the fort, and hunt for otter.

They found the village of Shee Atiká unoccupied. The inhabitants were at the summer fishing camps. Baranov boarded the *Yermak*. He led the Aleuts on an otter expedition to Chatham Straits. He ordered the other ships to await his return and the arrival of the *Neva* before they mounted an attack on the Kiks.adi.

On September 19, 1804, Baranov returned to Shee Atiká. The *Yermak* fired two rounds from six pounders. The *Neva* returned the salute and stood by to receive her long-awaited guest.

"Ahoy, the *Neva*. Permission to come aboard?"

"Granted, with pleasure."

"Alexander Alexandrovich, we were concerned for your safety."

"We've been in Chatham Strait on a hunt."

"Please accompany me to my cabin. I have mulled rum waiting."

Baranov slowly climbed the boarding ladder. He was a tired man. He took his hot rum with a sigh and eased into the captain's chair.

"Tell me, Alexander Alexandrovich, how was the hunt?" Lisianski asked.

"We took three hundred pelts, but there was no trading. We also sought the Kolosh from Shee Atiká, the devils who attacked the fort two years ago and recently attacked the *Unicorn*. I do not care for Captain Barber, her commander, but the point is the Kolosh have grown bold. It is my intention to punish them and rebuild the fort. These damned savages never miss a chance to kill a Russian. We can't even go outside the compound to tend to gardens and collect firewood except in armed groups."

"Why don't you hang the miscreants?"

"They are sly. We never know who committed the crimes. There is no leader. They are divided into many different clans. They wander about separately and independently. They're always fighting, even among themselves."

"It would be difficult to impose just punishment."

"Even if we catch the culprit, we cannot determine his clan. Some clans are friendly and trade with us, while some kill on sight, and that is constantly changing, for no apparent reason."

"Are there informants among them?"

"Seldom. Even then, you cannot trust them. They implicate one another, hoping we will punish their enemy of the moment."

"Perhaps intensive interrogation would work?"

"Oh, we tried that—even torture. They die without saying a word. It is just impossible. When we go among them, we never know friend from foe."

"How do you propose to deal with such intractable people?"

"The only way is massive generalized retaliation. If one more Russian is killed, we will shell and burn the nearest village."

"Don't you run the risk of uniting them? Such an indiscriminate policy would make you appear cruel and criminal to the board of directors."

"Do you have a solution?"

"If I may be so bold, I suggest we capture the minds and hearts of these people. We can kill. We can oppress and enslave them, but there are vastly more effective measures: education, inculcation of Christian values, and even intermarriage."

"In the meantime we must carry arms and live under siege."

"It will take time."

"It has already taken too much time. I do not give a damn what the board of directors think from their couches in St. Petersburg," Baranov said. "I have asked to be replaced."

"You have certainly earned the right to retire, but they say it is not possible to find a suitable replacement just now."

"When do you suppose they will?"

"I can't speak for the board," Lisianski answered. "By the way, in the Sandwich Islands an American sailor told me the story of the Kolosh attack on the Redoubt St. Michael. At Kodiak I received your request for assistance and left as soon as possible."

"We were not sure when you would arrive, so we tried to use the time for hunting and trade, but there was little game and no trade."

"Do you know why there was no trade?"

"I think all the Kolosh know we are looking for the Kiks.adi. They are afraid to offend either them or us, so they stayed away. We are ready now to attack the Kiks.adi at Shee Atiká."

"We have had a few brushes with them but have seen no large groups. They set upon us in the woods soon after we arrived. But we have seen nothing significant since," said Lisianski.

"They scatter in the summer to the fish and hunt. They will return to their winter homes now that the rains are starting."

"When do we attack?"

"As soon as the rest of the men arrive and the Kolosh are comfortably settled into their homes. We were separated from the main party by a storm in Chatham Strait."

"How did the Kolosh take the redoubt?"

Baranov did not immediately reply. The subject annoyed him. He reached for his empty mug. It was promptly refilled. Zakuski of salt, bread, pickled cucumbers, potatoes, and pork-stuffed pirozhki were set out. Baranov ate and drank his snack with exhausted, shaking hands.

"We were on good terms with the Kolosh. I purchased some land to build an outpost. Old Skayeutlelt agreed that we could settle here. The ol' bastard promised peace and brotherhood. For about two years, we got along fine.

"Things were going to hell in Kodiak. I received several reports of murder, rebellion, and sloth. Against my better judgment, I went there for an inspection. Some damned shaman in a white baidarka showed up there and incited the Kolosh. His name is Yaskadut. I suspect that he is behind all of these attacks.

"Well, anyway," sighed Baranov, "while the Promishliniki and Aleuts were on a hunt, these devils attacked, in the dead of night, during a holiday. There must have been about six hundred of them. Many had muskets. They even had falconets. Most of the Aleuts ran.

"The poor beggars in the redoubt never had a chance. The Kolosh sneaked in, found the powder magazine, and set it afire.

It exploded and all hell broke lose. They tortured and killed every man in the fort. They even pursued those who were fleeing, caught them, and tormented them in the most barbarous ways. Two of our Russians were crucified."

Baranov helped himself to the rum. "This is good rum. Much better than the poison we get."

Although he drank copious amounts, his speech remained clear, if slower and more deliberate. His hands stopped shaking. An ardent hatred for the Shee Atiká Kolosh still shook his voice.

"The bastards stole two thousand otter pelts and everything else of value that they did not burn. Apparently it was part of well-planned, coordinated attack on Russian positions from Yakutat to Kake. We must avenge our people and teach these savages a lesson or we will never be able to colonize this coast. But I am tired. I must get some rest. Tomorrow we will reconnoiter."

At dawn, Baranov and Lisianski sailed in the Yermak with ten baidarki. They crossed Shee Atiká Sound to the north, well above the village.

*   *   *

Yaskadut lay on a carpet of lichen, high atop his mountain. He gazed down upon the village of Shee Atiká, then rolled on his back and watched clouds play overhead.

He felt a presence and glanced at the sound. He started: there was a ship making its way to the shore above the village! Several baidarki accompanied the ship. He swooped down the slope in great bounds, like some wounded bird of prey. His feet slid with each step on large pieces of flat gray rock that skidded with the impact, adding speed to his perilous descent. Deftly he leaped from stone to stone until he struck one that did not give. He tumbled and rolled, cutting himself on the sharp stones, but jumped to his feet and continued his desperate race to his beloved village.

"Natook! Natook attacks! Hide in the woods."

YaḴwáan balked. "Why must we run like children? We should stay and fight."

"If we stay, they will shell us! They have cannon! They will bring more ships and more cannon. We will lose, and they will enslave our women and children. We will fight, but not now. We must catch them in the woods. We must kill and run. We must ambush and kill and ambush and kill. If we stand and fight with their ships, we will die."

The Tlingit grabbed what they could. The women and children scattered. The warriors hid.

The Russians landed a scouting party that crept along the shore under the guns of the *Yermak*. The Aleuts, led by Promishliniki, slunk toward Shee Atiká. They stopped short of the village, wary. Not a soul was in sight. They decided the Kolosh were at their summer fishing camps. The *Yermak* sailed to within four hundred yards of the village, then opened fire. The shelling went on for hours. The houses were stoutly built; several direct hits were required to knock down the walls and cave in the roofs. Eagle's Nest was the last to fall. The totem pole, Fog Woman, was cut down and dismembered.

Baranov and Lisianski led a party of men in longboats to complete the destruction. Lisianski examined half a dozen elaborately carved burial boxes set twenty feet above ground on decorated poles. He took souvenirs: weapons, utensils, and personal possessions from the dead. Ceremonial and battle masks were taken from the ruins of the homes. Eagle's Nest was entered and looted.

Baranov ordered the village burned to the ground. The charred remains were scattered. The Aleuts found food stashes hidden in the woods behind the village. They destroyed what they could not take. The Tlingit lay in the woods, watching. They saw the desecration of their homes, totems, and dead.

Lisianski and his men moved into the woods to the south.

"They were here. The food left out—they ran," muttered Baranov.

"I want to reconnoiter," announced Lisianski.

"Careful, Yurii Andreevich. The Kolosh are near."

"I'll take Arbuzov and ten men. We'll stay close to the shore and return in two hours."

Yurii, Lieutenant Arbuzov, and ten sailors armed with British flintlocks disappeared into the trees. Along the shore the forest was choked with underbrush and snags. It was difficult to penetrate more than a hundred yards. Gradually, though, the underbrush gave way and they entered the open garden of an ancient forest. Yurii was awed by the immense spruce trees. They trod on a peat moss carpet ornamented with ferns. Mottled sunlight defined shadows. Mist glinted through sunshine and shade. The men snaked through lichen-covered trees, brush, ferns, and devil's clubs. They moved in cathedral silence.

They could see no more than twenty feet through numinous shadows. The dark forest became oppressive. Yurii took up the rear. The hair was standing up on his neck. He passed an order to return to the shore, and the line halted.

Suddenly, flashes of musket fire erupted from all sides. War whoops, yells, and screams filled the air. The attack came from every direction. The enemy, wearing hideous masks, darted among the trees. They appeared and disappeared, dreadful visions of nightmare creatures, crazed by the destruction of their village and sacred totems.

The Russian line folded. Stumbling toward Yurii, they fired, rammed home unprimed shot, and spilled powder from touch pans. Gun smoke hung in the air. Tlingit appeared from behind trees and bushes, thrusting spears, firing arrows and muskets. Yurii screamed for a perimeter but there were no battle lines. The Tlingit appeared from inside trees and behind bushes, fired and struck blows, then disappeared. It was impossible to see them in the shadows.

A Russian reeled down the trail, blood gushing across a bewildered smile. Bayonets, sabers, war clubs, and lances slashed and parried in shadow and sunlight. Tlingit dropped from trees, popped up underfoot, burst forth from the rocks and bushes they had known since childhood. It was a grunting struggle for survival of thrusts, stabs, kicks, bites, and gouges. Iron, stone, wood, and bone clashed, crunched, and shattered.

Yaskadut was between the shore and the Russians. He waited, concealed by brush at the base of a giant spruce. Yurii placed his back against the same tree and yelled for his men to do likewise. He did not see or hear Yaskadut strike with a war club. Its iron-weighted elbow glanced off Yuri's head. He fell to his knees, pitching forward. Yaskadut pulled his obsidian skinning knife as he grabbed Yuri's hair.

A pistol ball struck the tree just above Yaskadut's head. Lieutenant Arbuzov cocked his second pistol and took aim. Yaskadut somersaulted directly at his attacker and the shot went high. Yaskadut rolled to his feet and thrust Aataagliga's iron lance through Arbuzov's sternum.

CHAPTER SIXTEEN

Chaos and Retreat

The rain stopped. Yurii opened his eyes. He lay staring up through the trees. Swirling clouds composed faces and animals. He was a child lying in green fields. Birds sang. A jewel glistened in his eye. A sunlit raindrop dangled from a fern, twinkling through an array of color from diamond white through ruby red and sapphire blue. Gems sparkled in and out of existence. Random thoughts effervesced: *Is this evidence of a perfect order created by God, or does this wonder and beauty emanate from within? Does man perceive order where there is only chaos? Can he conceive of anything else? Will he ever know? Is there an answer? Does it matter?*

The raindrop fell.

"How many do you see?" Dr. Liband held up three fingers.

"Three."

"Good. Who am I?"

"Dr. Liband."

"Where are you?"

"On board the *Neva*."

"Do you know what day it is?"

"No. How long have I been here?"

"Three days. Lie still. You'll be all right."

"Thank you." After a long pause, Yurii asked, "How many did we lose?"

"Three dead: Arbuzov, Seaman Havreelov, and Seaman Kvashneen. Several wounded. Arbuzov saved your life."

"How?"

"The leader of the pack was about to cut your throat. Arbuzov fired at him, drawing the devil down upon himself."

Tears came to Yurii's eyes. He faced the bulkhead.

"I was a fool. How many wounded?"

"Five—two grievously."

Yurii had a headache. He could feel several stitches in the back of his head, and he was dizzy when he stood. He moved slowly about the deck. He returned to his cabin to write a letter to Arbuzov's family and recommend a posthumous medal of valor. Arbuzov had been an excellent officer, full of life. Yurii remembered how playful he had been with the women of the Sandwich Islands. It was Pavel Arbuzov who performed a Cossack dance on the ship's railing when they crossed the equator. The letter was difficult.

Father Gideon came to see Lisianski. He mentioned Baranov.

"Captain, I wish to discuss Alexei Alexandrovich with you."

"Yes. What is it?"

"He sits and drinks rum for days at a time."

"Well, what else is there to do when the rain pours for months?"

"But he is becoming a drunk. He talks of nothing but revenge on the Kolosh. He has been brutal in his abuses of the Aleuts and the Promishliniki. He orders knouting and even executions without consulting anyone."

"Here, he is the only authority. There are no courts here. The only system of law is brute force. The Company was given a free hand in its charter to conduct court and wage war. You know that."

"I think he is becoming dangerously obsessed with the Kolosh."

"He has been here among a rude and uncivilized race for a long time. He has daily intercourse with a dissolute and licentious rabble. On occasion, in order to insure his safety and the survival of the Company, it has been necessary for him to resort to harshness," Lisianski said. "It is probably true that this long travail has blunted his finer feelings and rendered him less alive to the voice of compassion and philanthropy, but what is there to be done?"

"Perhaps it is time to recommend that he retire. He has earned it," Father Gideon suggested.

"He himself has asked for that, indeed begged for it. But the Company is not ready to replace him. He is old. His health is poor. His decline has been hastened by the shameful conduct of the people under him. He is not personally to blame for all the abuse."

"He is an absolute autocrat. As the undisputed leader of the Company in Alaska, he is responsible for the conduct of all the men under his command," said the priest.

"He must preside over a great number of cronies. They are under his care and a long way from the fountainhead in the mother country. He must provide the want of regular institutions and the administration of justice. That is a heavy burden. Even if there is drunkenness and debauchery, he has maintained our presence here and produced great profit for the Company. I doubt any other man could have done as well, no matter how sober and sanctimonious."

"Why can't His Majesty Tsar Alexander send more administrators? There is an abundance of bureaucrats in St. Petersburg."

"The tsar is preoccupied with the war. Austerlitz was a disaster. Napoleon may march to Moscow!" Lisianski rolled his eyes.

"God forbid! I sometimes wonder how the government has time for anything else."

"They don't. But Russia needs the money the pelts provide. Do you intend to report your impressions to the Holy Synod?"

"Oh, no. I have not forgotten Brother Makary's experience."

"What do you mean? I am not familiar with the story."

"In 1794, eight monks and two novices were sent to Kodiak. They were the first. They were sent with the blessing of the Holy Synod but in the pay of the Company. Their purpose was to convert the natives and curb the Promishliniki. There was conflict. Some missionaries participated in mutinous behavior because of abuse of the Kolosh. Father Makary was one of them.

"He left his post without permission, traveled to St. Petersburg, and complained of abuses to the Holy Synod. They promptly reprimanded him for not following the proper chain of command. He was sent back on the same ship with Bishop Ioasaph in 1799. They all drowned at sea."

"I have written deploring the waste unwittingly created by some of the Company's policies. I have reported abuses and corruption of some of the Promishliniki, but I will not find fault with so great a man as Baranov. He has spent his life for the Company and Mother Russia," said Lisianski.

"I too admire Baranov. I would do nothing to bring him into disrepute, even if I could. But I am a man of God, and I regret many things I have seen done in the name of the Company."

"Why, then, do you continue to serve? As we say in Russia, 'If you fear the wolf, don't go into the woods.'"

"It is not the wolf that I fear, but the abuse of power."

"I don't believe the Company is pernicious. The directors and shareholders are noble people, well intentioned but unaware of the most severe abuses. On balance, it seems to me that we are doing a useful thing. Things will improve if we do not lose our way with concerns in Europe. I am sure that with peace, both the Company and the tsar will send more people of quality and education to civilize this place and bring Christian life to the natives. Of course, I share your views. I promise that when we return, I will press for reform, but we do not want to paint too dire a picture. Tsar Paul almost terminated the effort because of such stories. Tsar Alexander is even more the humanitarian."

Dr. Liband entered the room to see his patient and added, "Yes. God bless Tsar Alexander and Mother Russia. But during the shelling of the Kolosh village, I felt like a Roman conqueror in the desert of Judea."

"How did you feel when the Kolosh attacked us in the woods and killed Lieutenant Arbuzov?"

"Pavel was a shining example of the best that Russia has to offer. Of course it is a great tragedy, but can you blame the Kolosh for attacking?" the doctor asked.

"Hell, yes! Those dirty animals attacked without honor. Your fine German philosophy clouds your reason. You sound like a traitor."

"I am no traitor. I loved Pavel like a son. What happened to all your wonder and respect for the complex language and art of these so-called savages? Your patriotism clouds your humanity."

"We will save these heathen from their benighted state. Remember your Shakespeare, my friend: 'There is a tide in the affairs of men which taken at the flood, leads on to fortune.' The tide has come. What we do here is for the glory of God and Russia. By the way, you had better not voice those sentiments to Baranov—he will hang you for treason."

"Russia is my home. It has been the home of my family for three generations. We are loyal to our country even if we are of German descent."

"You had better keep your own counsel. Even I find your position uncomfortably ambiguous."

"Thank you, Captain, for the good advice. I spoke frankly because of our friendship."

"I presumed to caution you because of that friendship, and Father Gideon there is the soul of discretion," replied Lisianski.

*   *   *

"Yaskadut has been a false leader. We have lost our homes, our village, our possessions, and stored food. What did we get in return? We wounded and killed a few Anooshi. We should have defended the village. They were not as many as we. We could have killed them all."

"With whom do you consult, YaḴwáan, your asshole? Your advice stinks! The Anooshi would have shelled us. We suffered few losses in the woods. We killed them and wounded them. We captured some muskets and powder. We will hunt them, kill them, and take their weapons. We will live off our enemy and grow stronger, but we must be patient and only fight when we can win."

"That is fine, but where are we to live?"

"We must go to Eagle's Roost. There we will be safe from the ship's cannon."

"But Eagle's Roost is small."

"From Eagle's Roost we can attack the enemy at will and he cannot get at us. The Anooshi will never know where or when we strike. He must never be allowed to rest. He must never be allowed to sleep. We can attack him and return to Eagle's Roost, where we will be safe."

The Tlingit dared not travel in the daytime upon Shee Atiká Sound. They knew the Russians would return in force. Traveling by night with *Ptichka* in the lead, the entire village paddled north to the head of the sound and entered Chatham Strait. During strong contrary tides, they pulled into shore and hid, waiting for a favorable tide and darkness. After two weeks, they approached Eagle's Roost.

On September 23, 1804, an armed vessel was sent in search of the balance of Baranov's party. At 18:00 sixty baidarki pulled into view. A salute of muskets echoed across the water.

"Egorov, fire two rockets in reply," Lisianski ordered. "Hang lanterns on the topgallant yards. Others may arrive late."

At dawn, the near shore on either side of the anchorage was covered with hunting boats for three hundred yards. Lisianski armed the launch with swivel guns for patrol of the shoreline to protect the hunters. The encampment included hunters from Alasca, Kodiak, Kenai, and Chugach. Lisianski wandered among them. Several pitched tents made with skins and baidarki. The baidarka was propped on its side. A low awning was made with paddles and sealskins. Some built fires; others hung out clothing, collected kindling, or cooked. A few simply fell into exhausted sleep in the midst of the bustle and noise.

The hunting party had been eight hundred men with four hundred baidarki. Some had died, some had been sent home sick, others had disappeared. Three hundred and fifty baidarki came back.

Once the camp was established, the Chugach began writhing and twisting to the beat of an old kettledrum in honor of the *Neva*. The Aleut responded. An elaborate greeting ceremony followed as barrels of vodka from the *Neva* were drained.

The survivors of the hunting party continued to drift into the camp when an alarm sounded and shouts rang out. The Tlingit had attacked stragglers. A large party of the Promishliniki and natives launched their boats. Lisianski dispatched his jolly boat under the command of Lieutenant Povalishin. A small armada rushed to the north end of the bay to rescue the stragglers.

They returned toward evening. A baidarka had been attacked; the two men aboard were taken and their heads cut off and stuck on poles planted on the nearby shore. There was no sign of the enemy when the reinforcements arrived. In frustration and rage, Baranov vowed to pursue the Kiks.adi of Shee Atiká until every single one was destroyed.

CHAPTER SEVENTEEN

Refuge

With ebb tide, white water churned into Chatham Strait from a deep fjord. At flood, it returned past boulders the size of Tlingit winter houses. Eddies formed whirlpools with glassine walls three and four feet deep. It was impossible to enter the fjord except at slack tide. A river cut through a granite mountain into the strait. At the right moment, the Tlingit paddled hard through the narrow gorge formed by the cut.

A massive rock rose ten feet above the maelstrom, one hundred yards beyond the entrance. On the flat surface of that rock was Eagle's Roost. A palisade of spruce set on end and anchored in rock surrounded a blockhouse of yellow cedar. The only landing was a ledge that appeared at slack tide. An immense slab of cedar counterbalanced by a log protected a small entry hole. Guards patrolled a deck around the inside of the wall. The blockhouse revealed slits through which the occupants could fire at the landing.

The Kiks.adi quickly hauled their weapons, food, and belongings onto the rock. A small powder keg bounced down the ledge and into the river. The loss went unnoticed. The tide carried the flotsam out the mouth of the gorge.

At the far end of the fjord lay a vast glacier, its spring melt lacing rock faces. Both saltwater and freshwater fish teemed in the fecund brew. Seals, sea otter, and sea lions sported in the long, deep lake. A sweet water spring bubbled in the middle of the block-house. For generations, the Kiks.adi Tlingit had used Eagle's Roost as a refuge. They could live on the abundant food supply of the fjord indefinitely.

The *Neva*, the *Yermak*, and five hundred baidarki sailed north seeking the Kolosh. They entered the strait and worked the tide, dropping anchor when it turned. The heavily forested coast was a maze of inlets and coves, each capable of concealing an ambush on those in the narrow strait. War canoes could suddenly appear, run-ning with the tide, and sweep down upon the ships.

The Chugach among the party knew there was a Tlingit strong-hold somewhere near the northern terminus of Chatham Strait. Aleut baidarki formed the point as Baranov's party made its way slowly and carefully up the narrow strait. They expected attack around each jut of land as they pursued a desperate search for the Kiks.adi. Lisianski's crew was forced to man battle stations day and night. A surprise attack in the restricted waters could render their can-non useless.

"Captain, I see something!" yelled Midshipman Berg.

"What is it?

"Two points off the starboard bow, along the bank. Something caught in the branches."

"You!" shouted Yurii Andreevich. "See that thing among the branches? Go fetch it."

An Aleut in a baidarka immediately retrieved the prize.

"Look, Captain, it's a powder keg with 'Boston, U.S.A.' stamped on it."

"It seems we have found our Kolosh," Yurii noted. "The camp must be nearby."

"It looks like there is nothing ahead for quite a distance, sir."

"Maybe it was carried downstream for a long way. Drop anchor! Tell that Aleut to inform the *Yermak* we have found a powder keg."

Baranov, on board the *Yermak*, had sailed past the mouth of the river. When he was informed of the find, he put about and ordered the Aleut scouts to join him at the *Neva*.

"What do you make of it, Yurii Andreevich?" asked Alexander Andreevich Baranov.

"I think it is from the Tlingit camp. It is not waterlogged. They must be near."

"It could be from an American hunting party," Yurii speculated.

"I don't think so. It is too far north, and no one comes up these inland passages. The Kolosh war canoes would have intercepted them," observed Baranov.

"We should stop here and send a party up that river," Lisianski suggested.

"It can't be done," Baranov replied. "We sailed past the river mouth. It's shooting out of that gorge at seven knots."

"Well, we could send a shore party along the bank."

"It is worth a try."

A party of twenty Aleuts and five Promishliniki, led by Lieutenant Povalishin, landed and moved up the east bank of the strait toward the river. The *Yermak* provided cover. When they reached the river, they turned east toward the gorge. The ship could not follow. Four hundred yards inland, the party was stopped by the sheer rock face of the mountain. They returned to the *Neva*.

"Captain, it is impossible to proceed along the southern bank of the river."

"How about the other side?"

"The same. It is seven hundred feet straight up on both sides of the gorge. We'll have to wait for slack tide and go up the river."

"That seems to be our only choice. So be it," declared Yurii Andreevich.

"How do we know the Tlingit are up there?"

"I sent a man up a tree. He saw some kind of structure in the middle of the river inside the gorge. It's them."

The ship dropped anchor. The Promishliniki made camp on the near shore to await the change of tide.

*   *   *

"Captain! Captain!"

"Yes, what is it?"

"Slack tide, sir."

"Very well. What time is it?"

"23:30, sir."

"Tell Mr. Baranov that I would like to speak to him."

"He is sleeping soundly. Seems he had some rum, sir."

"To hell with that. I'll wake him." Lisianski strode to Baranov's cabin. "Andrei Andreevich! Andrei Andreevich!"

Baranov rolled over with a groan, opening one bloodshot eye.

"What in God's name is it?"

"It's slack tide. Time to go."

"It's the middle of the night!"

"True. But we will have to wait several hours for the next tide."

"Fine. We will wait. The Kolosh aren't going anywhere. They're trapped in that fjord."

"How do you know?"

"The Chugach told me. Sheer cliffs surround the fjord. At the other end is an impassable glacier. The only way out is down this river."

"As you wish. We will wait until the next slack tide."

"Make sure the watch is alert. Those damned Kolosh like to fight at night."

"I'll see to it."

At dawn, Lieutenant Povalishin knocked on Lisianski's door.

"Enter. What is it, Lieutenant?"

"We found the guards with their throats slit and twenty of the baidarki slashed beyond repair."

"Damn! There must be Kolosh in the woods. Does Baranov know?"

"Not yet."

"I'm going aboard the *Yermak* to talk to him. I'll take a boat and five men."

Baranov was still asleep, snoring lightly, when Lisianski arrived.

"Andrei Andreevich, the Kolosh have attacked during the night, killing two Aleuts and destroying twenty baidarki."

"They couldn't have come down that river," Baranov insisted. "There must be some in the woods. I suggest we place a spotter in the trees and fire on their fort from the *Yermak*. If we can get in close enough to the mouth of the river during slack tide, the four pounders should carry, but we need some soundings. It may be shallow."

"It's worth a try. I will move up the strait and set a bow anchor. With the ebb tide we can pay out line and drift back to the mouth of the river."

"When is the next tide?"

"Two hours. I will maneuver the ship. You place the spotter."

By 09:30 Baranov had the *Yermak* in place and commenced fire. The spotter reported that the first salvo fell short. A stern anchor was set close to the bank of the strait, just below the river mouth. The slack in both the bow and stern cables was winched in, placing the *Yermak* athwart the shallow river mouth.

"Logs! Logs!"

The ebb tide was draining the fjord. A number of spruce logs raced down the river end on to the beam of the *Yermak*.

"Quick, cut the bow line! Cut the bow line!"

The southerly current pushed the *Yermak* away from the bank and downstream. She swung in an arc from the stern anchor just as the logs swept by into the strait.

"Those bastards are there all right. Take the longboat with ten muskets up the river."

Slack tide was brief. Baranov's men rowed wildly to make the passage. They were within twenty yards of the mouth of the fjord when the current became so strong that they could no longer make progress. The boat hesitated, then stopped. Slowly it swung and then plunged downriver with increasing speed. It fell into one of the whirlpools and spun under. Nothing surfaced.

Baranov shook his fist at the fjord. "As God is my witness, I'll kill them all! Tell Lisianski that I want to talk to him."

Once again, Lisianski was ordered to repair on board the *Yermak*.

"I want to send a shore party up the mountain. We can fire down on them."

"Maybe there is a way down into the fjord from the top?"

"It is worth a try. We will send some light field pieces. Maybe they can set their stockade on fire."

Fifteen Chugach and Aleuts led by three of the Promishliniki set out to climb the mountain. Thick stands of alder, patches of devils club and dense undergrowth, fallen trees, and the heavy brass cannon slowed their progress. They climbed all day.

That night a double watch was set on board both the *Neva* and the *Yermak*. The draft of the *Neva* prevented her from setting anchor close ashore; she anchored in the middle of the strait. The Eagle's Roost was beyond the range of her six-pounders.

The *Yermak* lay closer in, but her cannon did not have the range. During the last hours of the dogwatch a shout was heard.

"Fire! Fire!"

A burning raft shot out of the river mouth into the strait. The current turned it south. It carried down upon the *Yermak*'s anchor chain, spun, and glanced along the freeboard from stem to stern. The raft did not break up as it skidded along the larboard beam and beyond. Fortunately, the fire did not spread. In a futile gesture, the *Neva* fired a broadside up the river. The shot fell short.

By noon the scouting party returned and reported.

"The going was difficult. It took us all day to get to the summit."

"What did you see?"

"It is a long narrow fjord filled by a lake. A deep glacier blocks the far end."

"What is the distance from the summit to the stronghold?"

"Well beyond the range of our field pieces."

"Is it possible to blast rock down upon them?"

"No. The stockade sits in the middle of the river, too far from the cliffs for that."

"Is there any way down into the fjord?"

"The walls fall straight down for hundreds of feet."

"Could we rappel to the bottom?"

"Given enough line, but if they spot us it will be a slaughter."

"Is there a landing?"

"A few feet of gravel at the base. We could land and set up a couple of amusettes near enough to fire on the fort, but it is strongly built."

"It is worth a try. The men could take baidarki and race out with the ebb tide."

"It'll be hell getting by their rock and down the rapids."

"Send the Aleuts. If anyone can make it, they can. We have to flush those devils or we will be here all winter."

"Maybe we could starve them out?"

"I doubt it. They have fish and game in there."

"What about water?"

"The place is surrounded with it."

"No, I mean potable water. That fjord is mostly salt water."

"We'll try the amusettes. We'll use heated shot. See if we can set their stockade on fire. Keep an eye out for their freshwater source."

They dragged 120 fathoms of line, six baidarki, and two brass amusettes, each capable of firing one-pound balls, up the densely forested mountain. Two of the six men did not return.

The four survivors explained.

"We waited for dark, dropped the lines, and started lowering the amusettes. Two men followed. At the top, we waited for pulls to signal that they were down, but nothing happened. We pulled up empty lines. They were cut."

"Didn't you hear anything?"

"Not a sound."

"What happened to the guns?"

"Gone."

"How are we going to get those bastards?" Baranov asked.

"Maybe we can starve them out?" Lisianski suggested again.

"If anybody starves, it'll be us. We can't stay in this strait all winter."

"Perhaps it will not take all winter. We can wait until mid-November, but then we have to get out."

A permanent camp was made and a siege began. The *Neva* returned to Kodiak to winter over.

Those Russians that remained made two more attempts to run the river at slack tide. The first met a fusillade of musket fire. The second attempt was made at night, with the same result, except that more men were lost. It was apparent the Tlingit were especially vigilant during slack tide.

One or more Tlingit would make night raids to destroy a campsite or a baidarka or kill a guard. No one could figure out how the culprits passed in and out of the fjord. They were not sure that they even came down the river. Someone thought he saw a white baidarka in the moonlight, flying down the river amid ice floes. Two more guards were found dead. The Aleut believed that a witch who flew in a white baidarka was killing them. They refused to stand guard alone.

Baranov waited to see if the river would freeze. When it did not, he ordered the Aleut back to their winter base in Kodiak. Thirty Chugach remained, with orders to fire upon anyone who came down the river. A few weeks into the spring, several Chugach deserted their post.

With the thaw the *Yermak* returned. The *Neva* remained at Kodiak to replace decayed spars.

From the mountaintop, the Promishliniki could see the Tlingit moving about the stockade. The siege continued.

One night a Tlingit was shot while coming down the river in a baidarka. He was not seriously wounded. It was YaK̲wáan.

"I want to talk to Natook," YaK̲wáan announced.

They took him to Baranov.

"How are you called?" Baranov asked.

"I am YaK̲wáan. I have come to tell you a secret."

Baranov looked at the gargantuan, evil-smelling man, and asked him, "Why do you want to tell us a secret?"

"I am the true leader of the Kiks.adi of Shee Atiká. I do not wish war with Natook. Yaskadut does. Many of the people listen to him. He will destroy the people."

"What is this secret that you wish to tell us?"

"There is an underground spring of fresh water that bubbles up on the rock inside Eagle's Roost. This spring is fed by a stream at the top of the fjord on the south shore of the lake."

"So what?"

"That is the only source of fresh water for the people when there is no rain. If it is gone, the people will have to come out and make peace with the Anooshi. Many are tired of war and seek peace, but Yaskadut will not let them."

"Will you show us where this stream is?"

"Yes. I want to save my people and destroy that witch."

"Is Yaskadut a witch?"

"Yes. He flies in his baidarka and he speaks many strange languages. Once he was dead, but he came back."

"We will help you save your people."

"YaK̲wáan is the friend of the Anooshi."

"We will remember that, but we prefer to be called Russians."

"Did you find the powder keg that I dropped into the river?"

"Yes. We found the keg."

During the night, guided by YaḴwáan, a party of Chugach dropped down the wall of the fjord. They found the stream among the ferns, laced it with crushed hemlock, and climbed out on knotted ropes.

A Tlingit child died. Three adults became ill. Another child died before they determined that the spring was poisoned. They were astonished: it was inconceivable that anyone, even an enemy, would pollute a spring to kill his foe. The *Yermak* and all the hunters waited for the Tlingit to come down the river. It was spring. Ice growlers crowded the surface.

When YaḴwáan returned to Eagle's Roost, Yaskadut was sure that he had betrayed them. He challenged YaḴwáan to personal combat.

YaḴwáan was relieved that he was not immediately slain by the entire village. He was much bigger that Yaskadut; he was sure that he could overpower him on the skin. A Kodiak bear skin was staked to the ground. The combatants had to keep at least one foot on the skin or be immediately executed. The warriors had a saying: "The knife seeks the breath line. The spear seeks the fat line."

They chose weapons. Yaskadut chose the knife, YaḴwáan a short-handled thrusting spear.

YaḴwáan had hated Yaskadut since the day he'd been flipped while trying to push him over the back of another boy. As they circled on the hide, YaḴwáan remembered the event and the bewildering speed of Yaskadut's movements. His throat was dry and he could not swallow. White-mouth took him, but his frenzy rose as they circled and thrust. Yaskadut ducked under thrusts of the short spear or parried with his knife. He bobbed from side to side and circled away from the spear. His eyes shone ruby brown. YaḴwáan grew frustrated and impatient. He lunged. Yaskadut ducked under the chest-high thrust, pushed Yakwan's shoulder around, and almost decapitated him with a left-handed slash across the throat from behind.

The people gasped but said nothing.

Yaskadut cleaned his knife, then, spoke.

"We must leave the fjord," he said. "We will all die without water."

"We can collect rainfall."

"This summer may be dry."

"How can we get out?"

"The men can go a few at a time, in the night, with the flow of the ice down the river," Yaskadut explained.

"What about the old ones, women, and children?"

"There is a way through the glacier."

"No one can go over the ice."

"I know a way under the ice and out onto the top."

"The people cannot follow."

"They must. The ancients traveled many days and nights under a mighty glacier."

"Where will we go?"

"Back to Shee Atiká."

"Why? Is it safe now?"

"Others may help us. If we die, let it be in Shee Atiká."

Five of the men drowned. Two were caught, but 293 escaped. Yaskadut led the old people, women, and children under the glacier. The entrance was under a waterfall. The ice cave ascended a stream that collected water from blue ice. The people crawled through tunnels that spiraled into translucent aquamarine rooms. They cut steps in crystal walls. They walked through silver cascades of water dripping onto gravel with the ping and splash of rain. The glacier groaned and cracked.

They gaped at a monster, a creature with wings extending the length of four war canoes. Two horns pointed back from the crest. Red eyes glinted a baleful shark-like stare. The reptilian head bore jaws of serrated teeth. The people thought it was alive, but Yaskadut cajoled them past the specter. It was Xietl's mate, preserved forever in the ice.

Those too cold and exhausted to go on were left. Children cried and women moaned from cold and fear. After two days and nights of continuous climbing, they emerged into a sunlit forest. The sun warmed the people as they began their trek to the sea. They paddled down the strait, into Shee Atiká Sound.

But there was no Shee Atiká. The village had been razed. Looking for a place to settle, they spurned their previous stronghold located on top of a rock island commanding the sound. That location had been impervious to assaults of warriors armed with bows, spears, and knives, but it was vulnerable to the ships' cannon of the Anooshi.

They anticipated the return of Baranov in selecting a refuge on the Kaasdahéen.[5] They chose a location out of range of ships' cannon. They constructed a walled rectangle surrounding stout houses. A pit was dug in the center for the women and children to avoid cannon fire. To seaward of this stockade they planted heavy logs laced with willows, forming a palisade. They restored two burned-out cannon and collected spent shot.

They had been trading furs for gunpowder with the few American and English traders who still came to Shee Atiká. The powder was cached in the woods along the coast of the sound to the north.

---

5   Now known to some as Indian River.

Baranov waited at the mouth of the river in Chatham Strait. During slack tide, he sent baidarki up the river once more. They reached Eagle's Roost without opposition, only to find it abandoned. They burned it.

CHAPTER EIGHTEEN

Siege

The *Yermak*, the *Rostislav*, and two hundred baidarki sailed down the Chatham Strait for Shee Atiká. A rendezvous was arranged with the *Neva*, the *Aleksander*, and the *Ekaterina* before the site of the old Tlingit stronghold. Baranov planned to build a fort on the abandoned hilltop that had been the stronghold of the Kiks.adi. He called it New Archangel. He would seek out and destroy the local Kiks.adi from that vantage point in Shee Atiká.

The *Yermak* arrived first and dropped anchor at seven bells, in ten fathoms, two hundred yards offshore. The ruins of the old Kiks.adi stronghold loomed out of the fog. A light was set aloft to guide the Rostislav and baidarki. After the anchor watch was posted, the crew turned in.

Muzzle flashes etched the stronghold, followed by two concussions. The shot carried away the main mast of the *Yermak*. Roused from his rum-soaked dreams, Baranov stumbled to the quarterdeck.

"What the hell happened!" he demanded.

The watch commander replied, "The Kolosh are firing canon from their stronghold on the rock."

Heated shot pierced the freeboard just above the waterline, setting off the powder magazine. The bottom was blown out. The *Yermak* sank in minutes. The water was full of dying men. Baranov scrambled aboard a longboat as it and the baidarki pulled for more than half a mile to get out of cannon range. Men in the water who were prevented from coming ashore by the waiting Tlingit died of drowning or hypothermia.

The firing stopped. A sullen quiet fell as the survivors waited for dawn. Then screams started. The Kolosh were torturing those who swam ashore. Baranov and his men listened in impotent silence as they waited for reinforcements and dawn. Firelight silhouetted dancing ghouls cutting men to pieces or throwing them into the flames.

The flotilla grew during the night as stragglers joined Baranov. He choked on his rage, realizing that the Kiks.adi of Shee Atiká, in his absence, had recovered the cast-iron six-pounders from the redoubt at St. Michael, restored them, collected spent shot, obtained powder from somewhere, and learned to use the cannon—with deadly accuracy.

Outraged, frustrated, and still drunk, Baranov's face contorted as his body twitched. He waited impatiently for the balance of the fleet. All night he listened to the death agony of his captured men. Curses of the unwilling witnesses were muffled by the fog.

A dull silence greeted the first light. The Chugach began to murmur as they pointed to the shore. Baranov raised a spyglass and immediately threw it into the sea. Etched in his brain were a dozen poles topped by heads. The Tlingit stood on shore jeering at their enemy as they hoisted heads and impaled torsos on spikes.

The sails of the *Neva* broke the horizon, and a cheer went up from the baidarki and longboat. Soon, the *Aleksander*, *Ekaterina*, and *Rostislav* were also visible. The ships converged as Baranov was taken aboard the *Neva*.

"Andrei Andreevich, what happened?" asked Lisianski.

"These heathen sons of bitches sank the *Yermak*."

"But how?"

"They had cannon up on that rock we thought was abandoned. We must attack immediately."

"But what is the situation? What is the battle plan?"

"We don't need a battle plan. We outnumber them twenty to one. Bring the *Neva* in range and open fire on the bastards. I'll send the hunters ashore to clean them out," shouted Baranov. Spittle flew from his twisted lips. His body shook as he yelled at the hunters and pointed to the fort. "Attack! Attack! Attack!"

He stood in the bow of his longboat as it was rowed to shore, vainly firing his brace of pistols.

Lisianski reluctantly maneuvered the *Neva* into position to fire broadsides at the old stronghold. The Aleuts noticed something odd about the two eight-foot cannon visible in the ruins, but merely exchanged glances. They had long since learned not to speak unless a Russian spoke first. After a dozen rounds of unanswered fire, the *Neva* fell silent. Lisianski raised his glass and saw only splintered logs.

Baranov and his men gained the shoreline with no resistance. As soon as they left their boats, a disciplined crossfire of small arms stung them. Baranov was struck in the arm. The Kolosh had hidden among the rocks. Immediately after firing, they ran from the beach, beyond the stronghold, and into the forest.

The Promishliniki overran the stronghold, but found nothing. The Kolosh had moved their 1,250-pound cannons during the night. They left carved and blackened eight-foot logs in their place.

Baranov's force dared not pursue the Kolosh into the forest. He was assisted back to the Neva. Lisianski greeted him.

"You are hit."

"Yes. It is nothing. I just need a little rest."

"Please. Allow Dr. Liband to care for you in my cabin."

"We must press the attack! We have the vipers and their brood trapped! There is no way through those woods! I want you to take charge and eradicate the bastards!"

"It is almost nightfall. We will flush them out in the morning."

"No! You will attack now!"

"With all due respect, Director Baranov, I will not order my men into that wood at night."

"I order you to attack now!"

"To attack would be suicide. We have lost men enough for one day."

"I will report this insubordination to the tsar and the board of directors!"

"Report me to God, but I will not sacrifice my men to save your career!"

"How very admirable, Captain," Baranov sneered, "but if those Kolosh get away, you will lose more than your career. You will be shot for cowardice in the face of the enemy!"

"I will personally lead the attack—at dawn."

At dawn Lisianski took two six-hundred-pound swivel guns ashore. Each fired a one-and-a-half-pound ball. They were placed on the recaptured hill in the ruins of the old fort, commanding the village and the roadstead. Several field pieces were brought within range of the woods. The men were deployed in a crescent-shaped line, enfolding the field pieces. The swivel guns lobbed explosive shells while the field pieces raked the wood with grapeshot. The line advanced along the shoreline, flanked on the left by steep mountains and on the right by the bay. They combed the woods to drive the

Kolosh into the river at their backs. By the end of the day, not one Kolosh was sighted.

The lookout yelled, "Deck there! War canoe."

"Where away?"

"Three points off the larboard bow among the islands."

"Range?"

"Two miles."

"Lieutenant Povalishin, take the launch and attack!"

Povalishin flashed a grin and lowered the *Neva's* boat. There was a favorable breeze. The launch closed—hand over fist. The bow swivel gun touched off gunpowder in the baidar. Water, wood, weapons, and body parts blasted high into the air. Of the twenty occupants, all the bravest and best of the Kiks.adi, only four survived—each mortally wounded. By probing the wounds, the Russians learned that they had been to Kootznahoo, where they traded furs for American powder and flint. A prisoner was also persuaded to tell them that Yaskadut had been aboard but left the war canoe in his qayaq *Ptichka* when they reached open water. The prisoner died, but not before he told his tormentors that the gunpowder was intended for use at the new stockade built by the Kiks.adi near the Kaasdahéen River.

The stockade was set back from the shoreline and well protected by mudflats in the bay. The *Neva*, unable to sail in the light winds and shallow water, kedged into firing position.

The helmsman yelled, "What is that?"

"It's a redoubt," answered the lookout.

"But what is it doing here? My God, the Kolosh built it. Look! There are cannon in the embrasures. Where did they come from? Drop anchor," ordered Yurii Lisianski.

"What is going on, Fedorovich?" Baranov was still furious. He was not even courteous in his speech.

"Looks like the Kolosh have another surprise for us. They recovered the six-pounders from Shee Atiká and placed them in this stockade."

"Once again, we face our own cannon."

"Perhaps not. I see a flag of truce over the fort."

"Raise a white flag!"

"Aye, aye, sir."

"Let's see what they want."

Yurii Fedorovich was not surprised when a baidar with a white flag set out for his ship. When it approached to within easy hailing distance, it stopped.

Yurii knew that the Tlingit exchanged hostages when negotiating peace. Such hostages were called *kuwakan*, a word meaning "friendship." No one harmed them. Their captors danced for them, and they returned the courtesy. Humorous songs were sung, but every word and gesture of the hostage was followed closely to discern if peace was really intended. There were taboos for the kuwakan. He could not eat certain foods or indulge in sex. His captors knew this but frequently tested his resolve, telling him that his willingness to accept their gifts was proof of his peaceful intentions. They tempted him, taunted him, and watched his reaction closely for a sign of the truth.

Yurii demanded hostages before he would negotiate. This did not alarm the Tlingit. This was familiar. They would exchange kuwakan. The negotiations to negotiate began.

"I want the sons of five of your household chiefs," Yurii demanded.

A colossal Tlingit, called Dax,quwade'n, stood in the bow of the baidar and spoke for the Tlingit:

"We will exchange three firstborn sons for five Russian lieutenants."

"We will exchange two Promishliniki for two sons," Lisianski responded.

"We will exchange one son for two Promishliniki," Dax,quwade'n countered.

"Of which house is this son?"

"Eagle's Nest."

"Done."

Lisianski grinned. He knew that was Yaskadut's house.

Dax,quwade'n smiled. Even if the boy was a nephew of Yaskadut, he was only one, and no harm would come to him. No people of honor would harm a kuwakan. The Tlingit never learned that their two hostages were Buriat felons.

Dax,quwade'n negotiated for the Tlingit. Every morning, he arrived in a baidar alongside the *Neva*. Every morning, the Russians invited him aboard, and every morning, he refused, insisting that they negotiate with him while he stood in his baidar. Sometimes he made concessions. Sometimes he demurred, saying that he had to confer with the Kiks.adi. When trapped in a position, he withdrew for "consultations" with his peers. Frequently, he insisted that he could not speak for all Tlingit, that he spoke only for the Kiks.adi of Shee Atiká. As the negotiations became tedious, the Russians concluded that the Kiks.adi were stalling while preparing for a massive united attack.

Rumors of Tlingit coalitions had persisted since the May 1802 attack on the settlement of Kuskov. The Kiks.adi had savaged Redoubt St. Michael in June. These attacks lent veracity to the warning of an old Yakutat Kolosh that the principal chiefs from the Haida, Wrangell Tlingit, Kuiu, and Kake had met at Kootznahoo and agreed to help the Shee Atiká Kiks.adi destroy all Russians, Aleuts, and Chugach.

Kaniagit, chief of a village on the Prince of Wales Archipelago, offered to furnish all the powder necessary for the fight. Foreign interests, competing for the furs, supplied Kaniagit with powder, muskets, and cannon. The plan was known in Shee Atiká, Chilkat, and Yakutat. There would be more than five thousand warriors.

Negotiations droned on for several days. In the meantime, Baranov had sufficiently recovered from his wound to issue angry demands: One, the Kolosh must vacate their latest fortified position. Two, the Kolosh must sign a peace treaty, yielding Shee Atiká, in perpetuity, as a hunting and trading center to the Russians. And three, the terms of surrender must be accepted within twenty-four hours or the Russians would commence shelling the fort, after killing the hostage.

The Tlingit were appalled. It was unimaginable that anyone would kill a kuwakan. They realized the Russians did not value theirs. Messengers were dispatched in various directions. Yaskadut requested time to collect the Kiks.adi. He explained that he could not make such decisions for all the people; they would have to meet and discuss it. Those not consulted would not be bound. He told the Russians that the gathering of the Kiks.adi should not alarm them, for it was only to discuss the terms of surrender.

Baranov, believing that the messengers were sent to summon help, pressed the demand and refused to grant more than twenty-four hours. Yaskadut, desperately needing time, responded that he personally would replace the hostage for the three days requested. Baranov was so delighted at the prospect of having Yaskadut within his grasp that he acceded. Dax,quwade'n and the others protested. Yaskadut was much more important to the survival of the Kiks.adi of Shee Atiká than a mere boy. They urged Yaskadut to reconsider, given the Russian threat to kill the kuwakan. Yaskadut reminded them of the words of Tl'anaxe'eda'kwaa: He had been told he would be a great warrior—and he was not yet, he laughingly argued. He said he was assured: "No mortal, nor even the jaws of death, shall subdue thee."

He urged, "The prophecy must be fulfilled. Remember, the death of a warrior is nothing. The people must survive and carry the spirit of the Kiks.adi of Shee Atiká."

"What will your death as a kuwakan accomplish?" asked Dax,quwade'n.

"Who knows? Maybe there is more powder and flint at Kootznahoo, maybe even cannon and shot. Maybe our old enemies will realize they will be next. We need time to see."

"Do you know that these things are true? Are they coming to help?"

"Who knows what will happen tomorrow?"

Twenty men paddled Yaskadut to the *Neva*. A drumbeat followed each stroke. A mournful song lent solemnity to the procession.

Once on board, Yaskadut was seized, stripped, and thrown into the anchor locker and chained to the bulkhead by an iron wristlet. Within minutes, the hatch was closed. Stygian darkness prevailed.

CHAPTER NINETEEN

Capture and Interrogation

"Director Baranov, what think you? Is our guest suitably ripe for interrogation?" Lisianski asked on the second day of Yaskadut's imprisonment.

"Well, let's take a look."

The hatch admitted a sharp beam of light into the gloom. The light cut through the dank air, striking Yaskadut in the face as he stood to meet his fate.

"The bugger is not even blinking."

"Do you suppose he's blind?"

Two red-rimmed, burning eyes silenced the men.

After a moment Lisianski muttered, "He looks more dignified naked than my officers do in dress uniform."

"Would you like to talk to the creature that almost took your life?"

"Indeed."

"You may, but I have a special interrogation planned for him. Do you know Director Zhestokin of Atka? He arrived from Kodiak yesterday. He swears that this Yaskadut led an uprising in Atka. We know he led the attack against you in the forest. Undoubtedly he was involved in the burning of the redoubt at St. Michael. He attacked the *Yermak*. He fomented trouble from Atka to Metlakatla. He tried to incite all the tribes against us. Zhestokin wants Yaskadut placed in an iron cage and brought back to Atka for public execution. If Zhestokin doesn't take him, I will hang him from the yardarm for all the Kolosh to see," announced Baranov.

"Mr. Berg, get some sailors to help you and bring the prisoner to my cabin with an interpreter. Keep the prisoner in chains," ordered Lisianski.

"Aye, aye," answered Midshipman Vaseeley Berg.

"Doctor Liband, would you please examine the prisoner."

"Certainly, Captain."

The interrogation commenced.

"I am Captain Lisianski."

"I know who you are."

"You speak Russian."

"Enough. Your interpreter is not necessary."

"Mr. Berg, post a guard outside my door. The interpreter may leave. I will speak to the prisoner while Doctor Liband examines him. I will speak frankly. I urge you to respond in kind," said Lisianski. "Would you like some clothes?"

"I will not wear Russian clothes."

"Here."

Lisianski tossed an apron of tanned skins at Yaskadut. It was fringed and ornamented with rattling bones and birds' beaks. Yaskadut smiled as he tied the thongs together behind his back. They had unwittingly provided him with the ceremonial dress of a shaman. Stripping him before he was confined was supposed to demoralize and weaken him, but the result was quite the contrary. In his youth, he had to go naked, even in the cold, as part of his training. He walked barefoot in the snow and rolled up in a single bearskin to sleep on the ground. These were purification rites, in preparation for battle or some great ordeal. He remembered his uncle's training.

"This was taken from the grave box of one of my ancestors at Shee Atiká," Yaskadut growled, staring straight into Lisianski's eyes.

"Forgive me. I did not know that."

"You are not the grave robber, then?"

"Some of the men found a few things that we thought would be of great interest to the European world. We merely wished to share knowledge of your people and culture with the rest of the world."

"These things were taken after you bombarded and burned our homes. If the other Europeans are like you, I don't want them to know anything about my people."

"I would like to know how you create the totem carvings."

"What do you mean?"

"Where do you get the ideas?"

"We just start working and it comes out of the wood."

"Don't you have preconceived ideas? Plans? Don't you think as you carve?"

"Do you think when you walk?"

"If you have no concepts before you start, the results are not really art, but accidents."

"Some people have more accidents than others. It is like walking. Don't think."

"But everyone can walk. Not everyone is a sculptor."

"Not every one walks the same. The Kiks.adi approaches a camp through the woods; suddenly he appears. Everyone is surprised to see him. When Russians approach, the animals, the people, even the trees know." Yaskadut smiled as he concluded, "Some walk better than others."

"Would you like something to eat or drink?"

"Thank you, no."

"Come, you must be hungry. You have been in that hold for two days without food or water."

"To eat your food would forever stain my face. Besides, it is not necessary."

"Why is it not necessary?"

"I will be dead soon."

"Maybe we will not kill you."

"If you were human, you would not. Humans do not kill kuwakan. But I heard Natook. I know my fate."

"Do you think the Russians are less civilized than the Tlingit?"

"If you mean domesticated—no. If you mean honorable—yes."

"What makes you think we are less honorable than you?"

"We did not come to your land to kill and take things. We did not burn your homes and molest your dead."

"We did not come here to kill and take. We came to share our knowledge, culture, and the word of God. We do not make war on women and children, but sometimes there are incidental casualties that cannot be avoided. Director Baranov fired on your village only after severe provocation."

"We did not go to Russia, peacefully or otherwise. We know what happened to the Koniag, Chugach, and Aleut."

"What do you mean? The Aleut have schools and farms. They are being educated and their souls are being saved."

"Our souls are not lost. They do not need 'saving.' The Tlingit learn to hunt, fish, and gather food. We teach our children to build canoes, baidarki, houses, and all the things we need to live in peace and plenty. We are not farmers. We do not need to learn to speak French or to account for our belongings."

"You must agree that we bring you iron weapons for hunting and self-protection. We have better tools to make your life easier."

"No. I do not agree. Your iron brings death. You kill more than you need. You make slaves of humans, to accumulate worthless things. Our ancestors lived here long before you came."

"Don't you want to live with us in peace?" asked Lisianski.

"Yes, when you are in Russia. We will not come to kill the animals and enslave the people."

"You are amusing, my friend. Do you know what a great people we are? How vast the lands and multitudinous the people?"

"I know that vast lands and multitudes do not make a people great. You have better weapons — muskets to match the bow and the club. You act boldly, knowing that you have a great army waiting in your homeland. But they must come across the sea in ships. We will meet those ships and kill all who land."

"We are as many as all the tribes of salmon," Lisianski warned.

"We have enough drying racks for you all," replied Yaskadut.

Lisianski stepped to the entry and mumbled something to the guard. In a few minutes the cook's assistant, Mitrofan Zeleneen, appeared with a bottle of vodka and some smoked salmon.

"Here's some salmon prepared by Tlingit."

Yaskadut merely grunted but began slowly to chew on a piece of smoke-dried salmon as he sipped a glass of water.

Lisianski poured himself a small glass of vodka, tossed it off, and offered one. Yaskadut waved it away.

"What's the matter? Don't you like vodka?"

"Vodka is death. It is the poison you use to take our intelligence and manhood."

"I assure you that was not my intention."

"The effect is the same, intended or not."

Lisianski got up from the small table where they sat and crossed to the door.

"Well, it has been most enlightening. Perhaps we will speak again."

"Perhaps."

Midshipman Berg and two sailors were summoned to escort the prisoner back to his anchor locker, where he spent the night chained to the bulkhead.

The next day Baranov and Zhestokin were busy reviewing the Company's take from the island of Atka. There was no time to interrogate Yaskadut. By evening, both gentlemen were in their cups. Lisianski took advantage of the opportunity to interview Yaskadut once again.

"We merely want to live in peace and share this land."

"Share this land? This land is our home. Why don't you go home?"

"I can't do that."

"Why not?"

"I am a captain in His Majesty's Russian Imperial Navy. As a young man, I was inculcated with certain moral precepts. One is to spread the word of God. Another is to bring glory and power to the motherland. Whoever is unable to offer his body, his life, his blood in the service of those ideals is unworthy. To pursue these goals is my destiny. I have no choice."

"Tell your leader that we will never live in peace with him."

"Why do you say never?"

"Our gods have spoken. We have no choice."

"Why don't you listen to reason?"

"Whose reason?"

"Your own, of course."

"We have met and consulted and we have sought the advice of our gods. We must do what is ordained," said Yaskadut. A smirk played on his lips.

"You should talk to these gods of yours again. You must not continue at war with us. You must change your minds."

"It is not for us to decide."

"Do you mean that everything is determined by your gods?"

"Yes."

"How do you know that?"

"You can never know that if you do not have faith in your gods. If you believe, then you can hear the gods. If you do not, you cannot. The gods tell us what to do."

"It seems to me that you can shape your own destiny."

"I do not substitute my judgment for that of the gods."

"We too have a destiny. We are a great people of the only true God. Our nation spans half the world, from St. Petersburg to Shee Atiká."

"Why are you here?"

"We are here in the name of civilization and Christianity to bring true faith and enlightenment to you and your people."

"You are here for land, slaves, and fur."

"Our primary purpose is to bring a Christian peace and prosperity to this land, in the name of the tsar."

"We had peace and prosperity. We don't need your christ or your tsar."

"Everyone needs Christ, the Son of God, the Almighty Creator of the world."

"We have our own gods. Your god did not create our world."

"You must accept Christ."

"Why?"

"To save your soul from eternal damnation and hell."

"You sound like Father Gideon. Do you say that all who do not accept Christ will spend eternity in hell?"

"Yes."

"Even people who do not know, who do not get a choice?"

"Yes."

"Babies?"

"Yes."

"Oh, that is strange mercy, to throw little ones in an eternal lake of fire. I have done many things, but I would not do that. You say your god sees all, controls all, and is kind. Why, then, is there evil? Does he do evil?"

"You must have faith and trust in His mercy. His ways are not those of man. They are mysterious and wonderful."

"He makes hunger, disease, and storms?"

"These things are merely of this earth. They are a tribulation to try men's souls so that they may prove worthy."

"Worthy of what?"

"He who believes and is saved will not perish but shall have life everlasting."

"My people were given a choice. We could live forever, but we could not have children. If we had children, we could not live forever. We are like the salmon. They thrive, but choose to die so that their children will have plenty of food and a good life in the clear streams of the land. We do not fear death. Why should anyone want to live forever?"

"But what of your soul? What happens to your soul?"

"My soul will inhabit the Milky Way until it is called to live again."

"You believe you will be reincarnated?"

"Yes. Don't you?"

"We Christians do not believe in reincarnation."

"Did not your Christ die and rise again?"

"Yes."

"That is reincarnation."

"Yes, but reincarnation only for the Son of God."

"We believe all are equal."

"You know a lot about our people."

"Once, on an island in a distant sea, I saw enough. Your priests warned of a great apocalypse. There were four witches who cause death and destruction. You have brought them. They are here."

"What do you mean?"

"They pass among us on the backs of strange animals, slaying our people."

"Who?"

"Disease—measles, smallpox, and syphilis; alcohol—that takes our minds and manhood; guns—that needlessly destroy; education and religion—that cloud our minds and steal our souls. Now you come before us and say, 'You should become a Christian.' Why? In gratitude? Take back your disease, alcohol, guns, and religion. We don't want them. We do not try to change your faith. You have your god; we have ours."

"There is only one true God."

"And he is yours?"

"He belongs to all who will embrace him."

"I'll embrace him. You embrace my gods."

"I cannot. There is only one God and he is a jealous God."

"You have come to conquer the lands, plunder the wealth, and even capture the souls of the people. Then you ask why we cannot live in peace. Who is the savage?" Yaskadut boomed out.

Lisianski was startled by the vehemence, the bloody fire in Yaskadut's eyes and the jeer on his lips.

"But you must listen to reason. We offer you peace and salvation. Please think about it, consider it, and discuss it with your people. As Father Gideon said, 'We await your reply.'"

Yaskadut did not reply. He sat stone-faced, staring into Lisianski's eyes. Lisianski met his gaze with the stubbornness of a Christian doing a good deed. They stared at one another for five minutes without a word.

"I should have killed you," said Yaskadut.

"In the forest? Why didn't you?"

"I hesitated. I was a fool."

"You did kill my lieutenant, and for that you will hang."

"How, then, will I talk about your peace and salvation with my people?"

"I shall do my best to protect you until there is no longer any hope for peace."

"Will hanging me satisfy your system of justice and reason?"

"Yes."

"The killing was an act of war. I came under a flag of truce. I came to discuss peace. You chained me and now threaten to kill me. You are not human. Humans have honor. You have no honor."

"Was it honorable to ambush us in the woods?"

"These woods, this forest? The mountains are our bones and sinew. The streams are our blood. The forest is our flesh. You take this land—we will die. You came. We did not ask you. What for? You asked us to join you. You married our women. You educated our children. You told us we could maintain our ways and live in peace with you, but your ways spread like a disease among us. People forgot who they were. They forgot their fathers and their ways.

Some changed their language. Was it honorable to attack you in the woods? You have iron, gunpowder, cannon, and ships—we have the forest. Yes, it was honorable."

"You may hang just the same."

"What is the purpose of this discussion?"

"I want to save your soul from hell."

"Why?"

"It will please my God."

"So you collect souls as an offering to your god?"

"Well, you could put it that way."

"I just have. You please your god. He smiles on you. You are not interested in my soul. You want to buy your way into your heaven. You are a scalp hunter. You will take my life to serve your justice and my soul for your religion. I have no use for your justice or your religion."

"May God have mercy on your soul." Lisianski rose and summoned Midshipman Berg. Yaskadut was escorted back to his jail, the anchor locker. He was greeted there by Zhestokin and two pockmarked Promishliniki from Atka.

"Ah. Our guest has arrived," Zhestokin said smoothly. "I understand you have been regaled with food, drink, and gifts by our good Captain Lisianski and his friend the Jew doctor. Well, Director Baranov has kindly allowed us some time for social intercourse as well. Gentlemen, please make our guest comfortable."

CHAPTER TWENTY

Torture

The Promishliniki threw Yaskadut on his back across a pile of anchor chain and placed an iron bracket around his left wrist. The bracket cut off circulation, causing his hand to go numb. One of the Promishliniki had a knout. He stepped back as his assistant grabbed Yaskadut's right arm and pulled it tight. The whistling sound of leather and wire whip terminated in a moist, flesh-cutting *thud*.

"We know all about you. You filthy cannibal."

Another whistle. Another slicing *thud*.

"So you fornicate with ol' women!" *Swish … Thud!*

"You instigated rebellion among the Aleut." *Swish … Thud!*

"You killed Russians." The stroke was twice as heavy. *Swish … Thud!*

"You stole a baidarka that belonged to the Company." *Swish … Thud!*

"You led rebellion and murder up and down the coast." *Swish … Thud!*

"You are going to die, you son of a bitch." *Swish … Thud!*

"Slowly, slowly, and by inches." *Swish … Thud!*

"We will show you Kolosh bastards what it means to kill a Russian." *Swish … Thud!*

The men exchanged incredulous glances. There were no cries, no moans—nothing. Zhestokin was concerned lest Yaskadut be dead. He stepped forward, held up a lantern, and lifted Yaskadut's head by the topknot. The lamp fell on unblinking hatred. Yaskadut had not passed out. His bloodshot eyes flashed malevolence. Zhestokin quickly dropped the head and stepped back.

Swish … Thud!

The knout laid bare the ribs along Yaskadut's spine. They moved as he breathed. Yaskadut lost consciousness.

"Is he dead?"

"Hope not. We'd better stop before we kill the bastard. There are plans to disembowel him with the Kolosh in attendance," Zhestokin said.

*   *   *

Yaskadut was at sea among the whale and dolphin, paddling along the Aleutian Islands. The sun rose and set—rose and set. Figures appeared in the distance. Xietl darkened the sky as he flew overhead. Once again Yaskadut saw Tl'anaxe'eda'kwaa. They embraced and rose in a graceful spiral into the stardust. Ol' Galweit appeared, holding the hand of Gaelgix. They beckoned to him. Tle'an cuddled him to her breast. Kakuas-Geti gently kissed him on the forehead as Aataagliga beamed.

Thunk! The sound startled Yaskadut. Someone threw an Aleut dagger into the locker; it stuck in the deck, within inches of his head. It was an act of mercy, but Tlingit do not commit suicide.

Splash!

"Man overboard! Man overboard!" The anchor watch roused the crew. Lights were raised. A boat was lowered.

"Where's the prisoner?"

"He is chained to a bulkhead."

"Make sure!"

Russians and Aleuts mobbed the hatch. Midshipman Kovedyaev held up a lantern. The only thing visible in the gloom was an enormous blood-splattered white feather lying where the prisoner had been. The Aleuts gasped and stepped back. No one said a word. Within minutes, all of the Aleuts had quietly left the ship, paddling for the Aleutians.

No one had ever seen such a feather. It must have come from a mighty bird. Dr. Liband carefully placed it in a glass case for preservation. The Russians were baffled. Nobody could explain how the prisoner escaped or how the feather had appeared. Later, some said Yaskadut was a witch who changed his form into a great bird to fly away. Others thought he was Raven, turned white, as in the prophecy. Everyone grew wary. They spent the night searching for the prisoner, or his body, between the ship and the shore. When Lisianski was informed that the prisoner had escaped, he quickly looked down to conceal an involuntary grin.

"How do you explain it, Captain? It seems like a miracle. No one could have escaped from the anchor locker. He was chained to the bulkhead," Midshipman Kovedyaev puzzled.

"I don't know how he did it."

"Some of the men think it was a miracle. The Aleuts were terrified. They thought he was a witch or a shaman, with the power to change his shape at will and fly. They deserted."

"The man slipped his chains and crept out of the hold, or someone forgot to secure the prisoner and then did not see him escape," said Lisianski.

"Zhestokin and his men swear that they chained him to the bulkhead. The watch swears that they kept an eye on the hatch all night," whined Kovedyaev.

"I have a rule of thumb: When faced with a choice of miracles, always pick the least miraculous," Lisianski replied.

Yaskadut could not swim. Green water closed around him as he spiraled toward the bottom. He heard the song of the humpback, and a leviathan rose from the depths, lifting Yaskadut to the surface. The whale swam to a reef and rolled Yaskadut off his back, just above the water's edge. Yaskadut coughed seawater and groaned. He lay on the rock in the fog until he heard the voices of the searching Russians. He crawled into the woods, found a hollow in a creekside bank, and collapsed. The Russians dared not enter the woods. It was easier to assume that Yaskadut had drowned.

Lisianski's interest turned to ways of attacking the Tlingit palisade. He was amazed that they could construct such an impressive fortification in so short a time. It sat on a curve in the steep bank of the Kaasdahéen. It was more than 100 meters from a shoreline of extensive mudflats, hindering near approach by a gunship.

It was necessary to scale a fifty-foot slope to reach the base of a wall of planks woven together with willows. Each plank was three feet thick and planted ten feet in the ground. The palisade incorporated octagonal gun turrets strategically placed at the corners. The southwest tower commanded the approach. Tlingit guns guarded the flanks of the walls with grapeshot. The tower housed guards with muskets, protecting the wall from attack by land. Each tower provided a clear field of fire along the flanks of the palisade wall. Portholes, loopholes, and barbicans were abundant. A well was set in the center of the compound, providing a more secure source of water than the nearby creek.

Through the field glass, Lisianski observed, with a wry smile, that the Tlingit had incorporated many features of the Redoubt St. Michael. The Tlingit had set their palisade at the maximum range of the ship's six-pounders, the biggest guns they knew. Because of the shallow river mouth and surrounding mudflats, there was no way to bring the *Neva* within range. None of the other ships' cannon could carry the distance.

Lisianski amused himself calculating the range from offshore to the palisade. The gunners could estimate the range to within a very few feet, but he liked his academic visits with Pythagoras.

On a calm morning, at slack tide, Lisianski rowed offshore. Using his field glasses and one of the *Neva*'s surveying compasses, he took a shot of the southwest corner of the southern-most exposure. He carefully marked his longboat's position on a navigation chart and drew a straight line to the corner. He rowed in a straight line to a point where the same corner was visible at an equal but opposite angle. The length of that line was 1,200 yards.

He drew an equilateral triangle. He then drew a line at ninety degrees to the base, bisecting the angle at the top of the triangle into two equal thirty-degree angles. This yielded two right triangles. He applied the formula for the hypotenuse of a right triangle:

$$a^2 + b^2 = c^2$$
$$c = 1{,}200 \text{ yards}$$
$$b = 1/2 \text{ base line} = 600 \text{ yards}$$
$$a = \text{unknown}$$
$$\text{Therefore, } a^2 = 1{,}200^2 - 600^2$$
$$a^2 = 1{,}080{,}000$$
$$a = 1{,}039.23 \text{ yards}$$

The gunners were right. The distance was beyond their maximum effective range. However, it occurred to Lisianski that he could build a shallow draft barge of sufficient strength to bear one of the ship's long guns. The 1,700-pound gun could be mounted on a barge that would draw only two to three feet. It could be brought to within range at high tide. If it were properly constructed, it could withstand small arms fire as a gun platform. Lieutenant Povalishin commanded gunners Feodor Egorov and Mosey Kolpakov, carpenter Ivan Korukin, and carpenter's mate Terentey Nekludov to cut timber and build the barge, at a discreet distance from the Tlingit palisade.

Yaskadut lay in the mud for two days and nights of agony. Occasionally, he squirmed to the bank of the stream, sucked water from the surface, and then crawled back to his grass-covered hummock.

On the morning of the third day, he heard a sound. *Tap! Tap! Rata tap tap!* A woodpecker rapped in the woods. Yaskadut glanced across the stream to see a black-tailed doe grazing on the opposite bank. He crawled to the top of the hummock. There was a deep pool. Steelhead swam lazily above the pebbled bottom. Water striders skated on the smooth surface. An eagle screamed. He heard the sighing of the wind through the trees, the bubbling, gurgling, tinkling splash of the stream.

The ancient conversation of the forest revived him. He remembered this place. This was the same stream, the same pool, the same grassy bank, where he used to lay on sunny days as a small boy. This was where he had been taken by the Koniag. The deer, the woodpecker, the steelhead were exactly the same. As long as there was a clear stream with a pebble-covered bottom and white billows of clouds rolling overhead on a sunny day, nothing else mattered.

He knew the answer to the question he had asked when he was a child: he had wondered why he could not always remain a part of the forest. Now he knew the forest and he were intemporal. He knew that the twinkling passage of their finite being would sparkle infinite variations.

CHAPTER TWENTY-ONE

Truce

Aataagliga pulled sharply on his big toe. "Get up! Get up! Got to go to work now. Sleep later. Later sleep forever. Not now."

The old man's face appeared above Yaskadut. His voice was clear. Yaskadut crawled out of the hollow and stood up. He was weak. He saw Dax,quwade'n in the distance, not Aataagliga. Dax,quwade'n gave a yell when he saw Yaskadut. Yaskadut wanly smiled. He collapsed into the arms of the friendly giant.

The Russians attempted several landings, but they were repulsed at the water's edge. They searched up and down the coast for a landing. Before they put ashore, they discharged several guns and muskets into the woods, where they imagined the Kolosh might be waiting. They dragged various fieldpieces into the woods.

With great toil and loss of men from ambush, they commanded a hill within range of the Tlingit palisade. They soon discovered that the shot simply rebounded off the wall. Made of planks and willows, it appeared flimsy. But, although it would bend, it would not break. The Tlingit recovered the cannonballs and returned more effective fire on the Russian position.

It was not possible to move bigger guns through the forest. Skirmishes continued day and night for several days. Neither side could mount a definitive attack. The Russian position was close enough to the shoreline to fall under the protection of the six-pounders of the *Neva*.

The stalemate lasted until the gun barge was completed. A cannon was mounted on the barge and moved within range of the Tlingit Palisade. Several sharpshooters, under the guns of the *Neva*, manned the barge. The cannon began firing and continued firing, day and night, for three days, as rapidly as it could be safely recharged. The heated six-pound shot set fire to the walls within the compound. The Tlingit replied with the shot they had. Their powder supply was exhausted. Their reserved cache was blown up when a lucky shot by the Russians hit the canoe it was aboard. It was only a matter of time now that the Tlingit palisade was within range.

Toward evening, Dax‚quwade’n appeared in the distance under a white flag. Lisianski, who was now indisputably in charge of the battle, agreed to negotiations.

“I come in peace,” Dax‚quwade’n began.

“I receive you in peace.”

“The battle has been long. Many have died.”

“Too long. We have no objection to a treaty. You must send your chiefs to agree upon the conditions. I warn you: if you reject this offer, your former treachery will be punished severely.”

“I will return tomorrow,” said Dax‚quwade’n as he left.

*   *   *

“We must hold on,” Yaskadut urged. “Tell them we are discussing peace. The big gun is silent. Perhaps a storm will come up and drive the barge away. Maybe the others will come.”

“Yaskadut, why can’t we run away?”

"You know, dear friends, that the old people and the children cannot travel quickly through the woods. If we are caught, the Anooshi will kill us all. Go back at dawn. Give them another kuwakan."

"They torture kuwakan."

"We need the time."

At dawn, Dax,quwade'n approached New Archangel in a canoe. The kuwakan sat in the bow. He was a young Tluk^{W}ax)adi slave from Lituya Bay. He was dressed in great finery to make him appear important. They sang a melancholy song as they approached the shore. On landing, the kuwakan threw himself flat on his back in shallow water. He remained there until the Russians arrived to take him and Dax,quwade'n inside their camp. Dax,quwade'n gave an otter skin to Lisianski and received a Russian blanket in return.

"Thank you for the gift and the hostage as a token of your good intentions. We will wait till noon, but if the leaders do not come, we will commence fire."

"The people are gathering now, but it will take a day and a night before all is ready."

"You have it. But, if they do not appear by that time, we will destroy you."

Dax,quwade'n returned to the sea. He planned to seek help from his in-laws. He paddled out of sight, heading toward the Kaagaawatann to the north. He would also visit the neighboring villages of the Chookanedei, the Luik Nax Adi, and the Duk Dein Taan.

He knew the Kaagaawatann would not approach from seaward. If they came, they would travel south down Chatham Strait, through Peril Sound, and across Shee Atiká Sound. There had been no word, no sighting. If a large force moved through those narrows, the Kiks.adi would know it.

Dax,quwade'n had no illusions. He doubted that the Ḵwáans would unite to face the Anooshi. They were all proud and independent people. They had an ancient history of rivalry. The Anooshi pressed none of the other red men.

Dax,quwade'n was inspired when Yaskadut informed the people that some of the Haida strongly favored attacking the Anooshi. They wanted to attack long before the enemy reached their homeland. Yaskadut had performed miracles in the past. There was still some hope. They needed time.

Before Raven's call on the second day, thirty armed Kiks.adi approached the Russian position. They wore full body armor with battle helmets. The helmets were thick single pieces of hard wood carved with grotesque faces of animals or monsters, combining animal and human features. Below the helmet were wooden collars covering the neck and the lower part of the face—thick enough to withstand the blow of a cutlass. The helmet had a mouthpiece the warrior could bite. The helmet, neckpiece, and apron were articulated with thick sinews. The armor was made of hardwood rods, covering the body from the neck to just below the knee. Under the armor was a moose-hide long-shirt. Heavy walrus skin was used for high-top boots. This armor was worn for ceremonial displays and during night ambushes.

The armored troops stopped just out of musket range. They sat in ranks, looking at the Russian position. They bore a white flag of truce. Captain Lisianski led a party of thirty armed Russians to the parley. He started as he noticed that the leader's left hand was missing. The figure sat next to Dax,quwade'n. The Russian party formed a single rank and sat down within twenty feet of the Kiks. adi front rank. No one said a word for a full twenty minutes. Finally, Lisianski loudly cleared his throat.

"Yaskadut, I am surprised to see you."

After a brief pause, a hollow voice emitted from a grotesque mask of a man's face contorted in pain: "No doubt!"

"I did not know that Zhestokin was beating you."

"Your solicitude is touching, Captain, but I recall that you and Natook intended to hang me."

Lisianski was amazed at the literacy of this savage. He spoke Russian with the verve and sophistication of a St. Petersburg courtier. There was something preternatural about this Tlingit.

"We can live in peace," he insisted.

"Yes, but on what terms?" Yaskadut rejoined.

"The terms are the same as those offered by Director Baranov. Number one: The Kolosh must vacate all fortifications."

"There are no Kolosh here. We are all Tlingit Kiks.adi of Shee Atiká."

"Two: The Tlingit Kiks.adi of Shee Atiká must vacate the hill commanding Shee Atiká."

"Agreed."

"Number three: The Kiks.adi must sign a peace treaty yielding the ground where the village of Shee Atiká once stood, in perpetuity, as a hunting and trading center to the Russians."

"We have heard this before. What does this 'perpetuity' mean?"

"Forever."

"The last time you made this demand, you threatened to kill the kuwakan and fire on us unless what you called surrender terms were accepted within twenty-four hours. Do you make the same demand now?"

"Those were not my terms. I did not kill the kuwakan."

"One of you did. Who speaks for the Anooshi, you or Natook?"

"I have been given authority to negotiate a peace treaty."

"We will yield Shee Atiká."

"You must yield Shee Atiká forever."

"We will yield the ground at Shee Atiká, but not forever."

"It must be in perpetuity."

"Only the sea, the sky, and the mountain are 'in perpetuity.'"

"Those are our conditions. We insist on all of them."

"This is a grave matter. We must talk to all of the people."

"You are the leader. You make the decision."

"I am not their leader. We have none such. I have been selected to speak. I must explain this 'perpetuity' to them. They do not know what it means."

"We are tired of your delay and subterfuge. You must decide right now."

"We cannot. Much death will follow if we cannot speak in dignity with our people."

"If you will leave two respectable people as hostages, we will give you until morning."

Two slaves were put forward.

Lisianski noticed their features and dress and knew they were not from Shee Atiká.

"No. We will accept no more slaves. We know what you have done. We know that you value slaves very little. The new hostages will have to be members of your household, the Eagle's Nest. They cannot be either slaves or women."

"You must wait until my family decides. I cannot make such a choice."

CHAPTER TWENTY-TWO

Surrender or Annihilation

"We cannot send them hostage—they kill hostages."

"We must stall for time. We need more time," replied Yaskadut.

"Who will you send?"

"My household will choose."

After a short discussion, two fine young boys volunteered. They were great-nephews of Yaskadut. He winced when they presented themselves.

"You know, don't you, that the Anooshi may kill you? It is not like we treat kuwakan. Humans don't kill kuwakan, but these are Anooshi, not human. They may torture you to learn of our strength and disposition."

"We know, Great Uncle, but it is better that we die than all should die."

Yaskadut placed a trembling right hand upon the head of each in turn and said, "Our gentle streams have turned to rapids. Go forth and die bravely."

At the end of the day, the two nimble boys ran from the woods and lay prostrate before Lisianski, who was having tea. His eyes widened as he saw what fine young fellows they were. He clucked his tongue and shook his head. Tears threatened as he mulled over what he must do if the Kiks.adi did not surrender at dawn.

*   *   *

Dr. Liband and Father Gideon were on the deck with Lisianski as the sun rose. Father Gideon spoke. "Captain, I want your assurance that no harm will come to those boys."

"Father, this is war. There is no time for your humanitarianism."

"But sir, these are innocents! What possible good will be served by killing them?"

"These Kolosh have been trifling with us. The deadline we set has passed. There are reports of war canoes gathering south of Kuiu Island. We must press our advantage now. Have you forgotten the slaughter of Russians at Ilyama Bay, Yakutat, Archangelsk? Remember Lieutenant Povalishin?"

"How will it serve our cause to harm these boys? They did none of those things."

"We have beaten the enemy, but he will not surrender. If we delay, we could be attacked by a great number of their allies. Many more lives, both Russian and Kolosh, will be lost. We must demoralize them. Teach them despair. The only thing they understand is force and fear. We must break their backs. We will stun them with mindless, senseless, savagery. They will succumb in sheer horror. They will lose the will to fight. This will save lives."

Shocked, Dr. Liband added, "Captain, I know you to be a humane and educated person. How can a good man such as you contemplate such an evil act?"

Lisianski expelled a long and impatient sigh.

"Morits, my naive friend. I haven't the luxury to debate my decisions with you. You only prolong unpleasant tasks. God and duty dictate my actions."

Father Gideon interjected, "Do not take the Lord's name in vain. You will not do this in God's name!"

"You will both go below, please," ordered Lisianski. "Make ready to receive the wounded in the event of conflict. Alexei Mutofkin, cut the throats of the hostages! Hoist their bodies up to the main yardarm."

That was the signal to commence fire. The six-pounder began to rock the barge with its recoil. The fieldpieces from the Russian position ashore commenced fire. Columns of men maneuvered at the edge of the forest on either side of the Tlingit palisade. After three hours of shelling, a huge white flag was hoisted on the flagpole in the compound. Lisianski replied by raising the cease-fire flag on *Neva* and an equally large truce flag.

Yaskadut, alone and unarmed, walked out from the palisade. He walked to the shoreline, where he stood, staring up at the bodies of his great nephews. He raised his voice in speech.

"I fight no more. When we first met, one among you made a great speech. Father Gideon's words were beautiful and awesome. We did not understand them. He spoke of monsters and animals that we did not know. Many people do not believe him, but many people do. They became frightened by his terrible vision. We have talked and talked among ourselves and the people want me to answer Father Gideon. Father Gideon has killed no one. He spoke from the heart, so let me call him friend and brother. I speak to Father Gideon as a brother. He called the giver of daylight, the moon, and the stars one thing; we call him another. The Giver orders all things. He gave us this fine day for a council. He took his wing from before the sun and caused it to shine brightly upon us. Our eyes are opened, that we see clearly; our ears are unstopped, that we were able to discuss and consider the words of Father Gideon. For all these favors, we thank the Great Spirit, and him only.

"Father Gideon, I call you brother for you and you alone speak and act as a brother. When you spoke to us, long ago, you asked for a reply. You requested that we speak our minds freely. I now speak for all the Kiks.adi. To speak freely gives us great joy, for we consider that we stand upright before you and can say what we think. I have repeated what you said. All have heard your voice and all speak to you as one man. Our minds are one.

"Brother, you say that you want an answer before you leave this place. It is right you should have one, as you are a great distance from home, and we do not wish to detain you. But we will first look back a little and tell you what our fathers have told us, and what we have heard from others.

"Brother, listen to what we have to say. There was a time when only the people occupied this great land. Their seats extended from the sea to the mountains and beyond. The Great Spirit made it for the use of the people. He created the salmon, the halibut, and other animals for our food. He made the bear, the sea lion, and their skins for our clothing. He scattered them over the land and sea and taught us how to take them. He caused the earth to produce berries and plants.

"All this he did for his children because he loved them. If we had disputes about hunting grounds, they were settled without the shedding of too much blood.

"But an evil day came upon us. You crossed the great waters and came on this land. Your numbers were small, but you found friends and not enemies. You told us you only wanted a small seat among us. We granted the request and you sat among us. We gave you food and meat and you gave us poison firewater and disease. You brought hunters to kill the sea otter people.

"The white people had now found our country, and our furs and tidings were carried back. More came amongst us. Yet, we did not fear them. They called us brothers. We believed them and gave them a larger seat. They told us to disband. They urged us to disperse and live among them. Some even asked us to become like them.

"Now they want more land and more furs. Our eyes were opened and our minds became uneasy. Wars took place. Aleut, Eyak, Koniag, Chugach, even Tlingit were made to fight Tlingit. Many of our people died.

"Now you are many and we have no place to hunt. You have taken the country but you are not satisfied. Now you want to force your religion upon us. You hunt our spirits.

"Brother, continue to listen. You say that you are sent to instruct us how to worship the Great Spirit agreeably to his mind, and if we do not take hold of the religion you teach, we shall be unhappy hereafter. You say that you are right and we are lost. How do we know this to be true? We understand that your religion is written in a book. If it were intended for us as well as you, why has not the Great Spirit given it to us, and not only to us, but why did he not give to our forefathers the knowledge of that book, with the means of understanding it rightly? We only know what you tell us about it. How shall we know what to believe, being so often deceived by the white people?

"Brother, you say there is but one way to worship and serve the Great Sprit. If there is but one religion, why do you white people argue about it so much? Why not agree, as you can all read the book?

"Brother, we do not understand these things. We are told that your religion was given to your forefathers and has been handed down from father to son. We also have a belief that was given to our forefathers and has been handed down to us, their children. We worship that way. It teaches us to be thankful for all the favors we receive, to love each other, and to be united. We never quarrel about religion. We respect each man's way.

"Brother, the Great Spirit has made us all, but he has made a great difference between his white and red children. He has given us a different color and different customs. To you, he has given the arts. To these, he has not opened our eyes. We know these things to be true. Since he has made so great a difference between us in other things, why may we not conclude that he has given us a different religion according to our understanding? The Great Spirit does right. He knows what is best for his children. We are satisfied.

"Brother, we do not wish to destroy your religion or take it from you. We want only to enjoy our own. We saw and watched to see if what you say is good. We listened and consider what you said and it appears untrue.

"Brother, you have now heard our answer to your talk, and this is all we have to say at present. As we are going to part, we will come and take you by the hand, and hope the Great Spirit will protect you on your journey, and return you safe to your friends."[6]

Zhestokin was on board the gun barge. An infamous duelist, he was especially proud of a brace of dueling pistols made by Mortimer of London. They had ten-inch barrels and fired a 15.7-millimeter ball. He raised the saw-handled butt of one, wrapped his second finger around the spur below the guard, and slowly squeezed as he trained the gun on Yaskadut, about twenty-five yards away.

"Here is your handshake, you red-skinned bastard," he yelled.

---

6   This is actually Red Jacket's reply to Missionary Cram at Buffalo, New York, in 1805. It has been altered slightly, but its reason, logic, and beauty belong to Red Jacket. The source is *The Gospel of the Redman, A Way of Life*, compiled by Ernest Thompson Seton and Julia M. Seton, Publisher Seton Village, Santa Fe, NM; Reprint. edition (1966) ASIN: B002K7MEI2

Just as he fired, a Chugach with a cutlass turned and cut his arm off. The shot kicked up dirt at Yaskadut's feet. A Russian shot the Chugach in the head. Yaskadut did not flinch.

This was not the response Yurii Lisianski had expected to hear. It was not what Father Gideon wanted. Infuriated by Zhestokin and frustrated by the stubbornness of Yaskadut, he boomed, "Yaskadut, I order you to surrender immediately or we will kill every man, woman, and child!"

"You will kill us all whether we surrender or not."

"We will give no quarter if you do not surrender immediately!"

"I personally ask for none, but my people must survive."

"You will have to trust us. Surrender now and we will spare you. If not, we will annihilate the Kiks.adi of Shee Atiká from the face of the earth!"

"I do not trust you. I shall never trust the European, but we will surrender. We will leave on the morning tide for other lands and a new home."

"No. You will leave now!"

"We will not. You will have to kill us all."

"I will give you until the morning, but I promise that if you are not out of that fort by the end of the flood tide, we will destroy every vestige of your memory."

"The people will confirm this agreement by singing. This will mean that we are leaving on the morning tide."

CHAPTER TWENTY-THREE

A GREAT SACRIFICE

The morning tide rose and began to ebb, but Lisianski decided to wait. The Chugach in the Russian force were now free to roam the woods about the fort. They plundered the Tlingit caches of food. Finally, Lisianski gave the order to commence fire. During a lull in the renewed shelling, the Russians heard the Tlingit sing, "Oo, oo, oo!" The Russian men answered with a rousing cheer of "Hurrah, hurrah, hurrah!"

A dirge rose from the fort as the sea birds went to roost. A drum beat a death march. Occasionally a falsetto expressed fury and pain. At intervals, there was oppressive silence—and then, another aching song carried out to sea. A drum measured the night. The Russians waited and listened to the death throes of a culture.

As night fell, a great fire roared and crackled in the middle of the fort compound. The flames flickered and reflected off shining eyes, jet-black hair, and burnished copper skin.

Dax,quwade'n stood and spoke to the people. "We must leave this place. We have no gunpowder."

"How can we leave? This is our body, our blood. We fought before there was gunpowder, before there were muskets and cannon," rejoined "X.atgawet.

"You are a proud warrior, great "X.atgawet. You gave eight potlatches like the eight bones of the body. Your Frog House is well known, but it too has been burned."

"We cannot leave our homes. We will stay and rebuild Shee Atiká."

Yaskadut joined in, "Dear father. We love and respect you, but we cannot stay. The Anooshi will kill us if we do not surrender. If we do surrender, we will become slaves. We will die the slow death of the Koniag. We will disappear among the scatter peoples like the Eyak or become dogs like the Chugach."

"If we stay, Xietl will bring a great storm and destroy the Anooshi and their ships."

"No, dear X.atgawet. Xietl will not bring a storm. I, Yaskadut, know. No storm will come in time to save us. We have no more time."

A great moan rose from the people and filled the night. The drumbeat started, and a shaman called upon the gods and screamed invectives at the enemy.

"Maybe the powerful Kaagaawatann, our brothers, will come from the North. Our neighboring villagers, the Chookanaidi, Luk Nax Adi, and the Duk Dein Taan, must surely have seen and heard what is happening and will come to join us. For, surely, they are next."

"They are just beginning to gather in the Strait of Keku, but too late. There is no time."

"Then Dax,quwade'n is right, and it is time to build a new village someplace else."

"X.atgawet, old father. There is greater sadness."

"What can be greater sadness than for the Kiks.adi of Shee Atiká to leave their body?"

"The Anooshi threaten our souls, our ancestors, our memories. If we fight, we die. If we surrender, we die."

"How do you know these things?"

"Don't you remember the story of the Koniag, the Chugach, and the Aleut? The Koniag fought and died. The Eyak fought and died. The Aleuts and Chugach surrendered to slavery, and their souls are dying. Xietl brought Tl'anaxe'eda'kwaa to me. She showed me the way. She told me of the sacred manner of the world and our way in it. Death of the warrior is not important. The flame of the people must live on. It is a precious light to be passed from one Kiks.adi to the other. The soul is the lamp that keeps the flame alive. We must preserve the light. We must preserve the people."

"How can we do this?"

"We cannot surrender. They will enslave all they do not kill. We must escape."

"We cannot go by sea. The Anooshi ships will slaughter us. The old ones and children cannot travel through the woods. The enemy waits there also. If they catch us at sea or in the woods, they will kill us all!"

"You have seen the salmon. They swim up the stream to spawn. They run a gauntlet of bear, fishhooks, gaffs, and traps. Many die, maybe most, but some live to spawn. Their flame does not die."

"We are not as many as the salmon."

"We can use the night, and Fog Lady will protect us."

"Where will we go?"

"Up the Chatham Strait to Chaatlk'aa Noow."

"When?"

"When the night rolls over."

"What if they hear us?"

"We must make sure that they do not."

"Many will die, perhaps all."

*   *   *

On board the *Neva*, the men could see a glow of the fire from the compound. Muskets fired. Shrieks and screams carried across the water. A vagrant wind blustered as voices and howling dogs filled the night. The somber watch listened.

"What in God's name are they doing, Captain?"

"They are just shamaning. We will see come daylight, if this damned fog ever lifts."

Most of the Russians passed the night on deck. They watched and waited as they drank tea, murmuring among themselves. Some talked of home. Others speculated about the enemy. All anticipated an end to the prolonged battle with the Kolosh. For two years they had pursued and fought these people from Shee Atiká.

It was agreed that they would conquer one group at a time. There was a continuing debate among the men about the possibility that the Americans might help the Kolosh.

"The Americans want the furs for themselves."

"True. But will they risk war with Russia to get them?"

"What risk? Russia will not conduct a war halfway around the world. She has her hands full. We just finished with the Persians. Napoleon handed us our heads in Austerlitz. Now the Turks are making noise. We are too far from St. Petersburg, and the *Neva* is the only real fighting ship in the Pacific."

"The Americans are already supplying these heathen with gunpowder and weapons. They will achieve their goal without fighting us. They will use the Kolosh."

"I also worry about the English. They are doing the same thing."

"Yes, and don't forget that the Spanish claim the entire west coast of North America."

"We are too far-flung. We have become the new Holy Roman Empire, and you know what happened to them."

"If the Americans continue to infiltrate Russian Alaska, we will have to do something."

"We need a much bigger fleet in the Pacific to defend our interests."

"My only interest is to get home to St. Petersburg. I want to stroll along the banks of the Neva with my sweetheart."

"Me too, but I don't call it strolling."

"Oh. You want to 'stroll' with his sweetheart?"

"Listen! They are singing again."

"You call that singing? How can they keep it up all night? They don't have vodka, do they?"

"Who knows what they have."

"Baranov knows. The way they beat that Kolosh before he escaped, I'll bet he told them everything."

"I'll be glad when it is daylight."

*   *   *

"Good morning, Captain."

"Good morning, Doctor."

"Any evidence that the Kolosh are finally leaving the fort?"

"Not yet. It would be better if this fog would burn off."

"It usually does around ten or eleven. It sure is quiet over there now. By the way, did you ever figure out what kind of feather that was?"

"No. I have never seen anything like it. It appeared to be a flight feather from a wing, but huge. It is much too big for any bird that flies."

"Where is it?"

"That is another mystery. I put it in a glass case for safekeeping. I wanted it examined by ornithologists, but it is gone."

"Gone? What do you mean?"

"I locked it in my cabin in a glass case. When I looked for it this morning, it was gone."

"Someone must have taken it."

"Of course, but who?"

"We will look into that when this is over."

Only the surf and the cry of gulls broke the silence of the morning. The acrid smell of smoldering wood degraded the scent of kelp and fog. The odor drifted from the fort to the *Neva*. The sharp smell awoke sailors from their drowsy night watch.

The sound of Russian Orthodoxy greeted the morning. Father Gideon blessed the sailors. There would also be an evening church service, just as there had been every Sunday since the beginning of the voyage.

"Well. High tide has come and gone again and there is no sign of the Kolosh."

Petr Povalishin stood next to Yurii Lisianski. He raised his glass and observed the fort for a full ten minutes.

"Captain, there is something strange. The stockade walls are lined with ravens."

Lisianski took the glass.

"You are right, Stepanov. On watch, do you see any movement?"

"Nothing, sir. Nothing has moved since the fog lifted," replied the lookout.

"Lieutenant Povalishin! Take six armed men ashore with the longboat. I want to know what they are up to. Mind you, proceed with caution. The gun barge will provide cover."

"Captain, may I go ashore with the longboat? You know that those people are in bad shape. Our shelling must have killed and wounded many."

"What are you talking about, Doctor? You want to administer to the enemy?"

"The women and children are not our enemy."

"Oh, yes they are. Their women and children have killed Aleuts and Russians. This is not a European affair, my friend."

"Nevertheless, I ask permission to go with the landing party."

"Granted," Lisianski said with exasperation.

Povalishin, Liband, and six armed sailors rowed through the last wisps of swirling fog to the beach. As they approached the shore, Povalishin hailed the gun barge, "Egorov! Provide cover. We are going to the fort."

The men from the barge trained the gun. One stood at the right of the muzzle with a sponge and rammer. On the opposite side of the muzzle stood another, ready to place the powder charge and ammunition in the bore. A third man stood to the right of the breech to thumb the vent while the gun was sponged. The fourth man, Gunner Egorov, stood by with the portfire glowing. The landing party halted within fifty yards of the gates.

Povalishin hailed the fort, "Allooo, the fort! Allooo, the fort!" They stood silently waiting for a reply. Nothing was heard. Even the ravens were silent.

Two sailors ran forward and swung open the gates.

The compound floor was covered with babies, the elderly, and dogs—their throats slit. Doctor Morits Liband fell to his knees. He pulled his hair and clawed at his face in grief and incredulity. He sobbed one word over and over: "Masada! Masada! Masada!"

AFTERWORD

Perhaps it would be better to let Lisianski's words speak for themselves as they appear in his ship's log:

"When morning came, I observed a great number of crows hovering about the settlement. I sent on shore to ascertain the cause of this; and the messenger returned with the news that the natives had quitted the fort during the night, leaving in it, alive, only two old women and a little boy. It appears that, judging of us by themselves, they imagined that we were capable of the same perfidiousness and cruelty; and that if they had come out openly in their boats, as had been proposed, we should have fallen upon them in revenge for their past behavior. They had therefore preferred running into the woods, leaving many things behind, which, from their haste, they had not been able to take away. By this unexpected flight we obtained a supply of provisions for our hunters, and upwards of twenty large canoes, many of which were quite new. Mr. Baranov ordered the fort to be completely destroyed; to effect which, three hundred men were sent on shore, with a sufficient guard, under an officer from my ship.

"It was on the eighth of October, 1804, that the fate of Sitca Fort was decided. After everything that could be of use was removed out of it, it was burned to the ground. Upon my entering it, before it was set on fire, what anguish did I feel, when I saw, like a second massacre of innocents, numbers of young children lying together murdered, lest their cries, if they had been borne away with their cruel parents, should have led to a discovery of the retreat to which they were flying! In addition, several dogs had experienced the same fate. —O man, man! Of what cruelties is not thy nature, civilized or uncivilized, capable? But I turn from this scene of horror to pursue my narrative..."

Conflicting accounts of what happened are still debated. Some Tlingit allege that the Kiks.adi stealthily sent their women and children from the compound to safety before the final moment. The titles of two sources illustrate the conflict: *The Tlingit Indians in Russian America, 1741–1867*, by Andrei Val'Terovich Grinev, and *Anooshi Lingit Aani Ka, Russians in Tlingit America, The Battles of Sitka 1802 and 1804*, edited by the Tlingit Nora Marks Dauenhauer, Richard Dauenhauer, and Lydia T. Black.

EPILOGUE

Yurii Fedorovich Lisianski (1773–1837) survived his circumnavigation, as did his stout ship the *Neva*, a collier hull with brigantine rigging that had been converted to a war sloop by the Russians. On July 22, 1806, the *Neva* dropped anchor at Kronstadt, completing the circumnavigation that began on August 7, 1803. She arrived sixteen days before her sister ship, the *Nadezhda*, a frigate, commanded by Ivan Fedorovich Kruzenstern. Lisianski was never forgiven for completing the circumnavigation before Kruzenstern, the designated fleet commander.

Yurii Lisianski achieved the rank of Captain of the First Order. He married the widow Charlotte Karlovna Zhandr, née Baroness de Brunold. They wintered in her house in Moscow, V block, No. 414, at the Semenovskii Bridge, and summered at the Kobrino Estate near Gatchina.

The second half of Lisianski's life passed quietly and without notice. During his rare visits to St. Petersburg, he strolled along the tree-lined granite bank of the river Neva, past a heroic statue of Kruzenstern dedicated to "the first Russian sailor to sail around the world, Admiral Ivan Fedorovich Kruzenstern."

Lisianski died on March 6, 1837, and lies in the Tikhvinskoe cemetery in the Aleksandr-Nevskii Lavra. A modest square monument bears a bronze portrait and an anchor with a broken anchor chain.

Ivan Fedorovich Kruzenstern (1770–1846) was born in Haggud, Estonia, on November 19, 1770, as Anton Von Kruzenstern. From 1787 to 1789, he served in the Russian Navy during the Russo-Swedish War, then served on a British ship in 1793. From 1797 to 1799, he traveled to the Indies and to Canton on a British merchant ship.

He commanded the convoy that is the subject of this book aboard the *Nadezhda* from 1803 to 1806. From 1810 to 1814, he wrote and published *Voyage Around the World, 1803–1806*, and in 1814 contributed to the *Hydrography of the Great Ocean*. In 1815 he led an expedition to the Arctic in search of the Northwest Passage. From 1824 to 1827, he wrote and published *Atlas of the Pacific Ocean*. In 1829 he was promoted to Rear Admiral and served as director of the Naval Academy. In 1836 he was promoted to Vice Admiral and in 1841 to Admiral. In addition to his statute on the River Neva, the world's second-largest traditional sailing vessel (a training ship for naval cadets still afloat) was christened the *Kruzenstern*. He died on his estate of Asz, near Revel (Estonia), on August 24, 1846.

After the abuses of the trappers and industrialists of Baranov's era, Yaskadut's people were treated humanely by an enlightened Russian navy.

The Tlingit are a proud nation, maintaining their ethnic identity. They are self-governing. Much of their land remains in their exclusive care. They wisely market their artistic works and zealously guard their legend.

The Tlingit Shee Atiká Kwáan survived by an act both terrible and magnificent: an act that few acknowledge, many deny, and none call brave—but it was. There are few things more difficult than death. Killing your children to survive, as a people, is one—living with that memory is another.